5-Minute Messages for Children's Special Days

By Donald Hinchey

Group®

Loveland, Colorado

Dedication

To Margaret, who makes each day special.

Credits
Editorial team: Christine Yount, Jennifer Root Wilger, Mike Nappa, Bonnie Temple, and Jane Vogel
Cover designed by Liz Howe
Interior designed by Dori Walker

Except where otherwise noted, Scriptures are quoted from The Youth Bible, New Century Version, copyright © 1991 by Word Publishing, Dallas, Texas 75039. Used by permission.

Library of Congress Cataloging-in-Publication Data
Hinchey, Donald, 1943-
    5-minute messages for children's special days / by Donald Hinchey.
        p.   cm.
    ISBN 1-55945-240-4
    1. Children's sermons. 2. Church year sermons. 3. Sermons, American.   I.
Title. II. Title: Five-minute messages for children's special days.
BV4315.H513   1994
252'.53--dc20   94-30673
                                                      CIP

10 9 8 7 6 5 4 3 2 1   03 02 01 00 99 98 97 96 95 94

Printed in the United States of America.

Contents

Part One: Messages for Fall

Part Two: Messages for Winter

Part Three: Messages for Spring

Part Four: Messages for Summer and All Seasons

Introduction

Making Your Messages Special

Children everywhere hope and wait and count the days as major holidays approach. Kids look forward to Christmas parties, birthday cakes, and family celebrations that break up the normal routine of life.

5-Minute Messages for Children's Special Days contains 52 active experiences you can lead children through that acknowledge and commemorate special days in a child's calendar. Children will build a "people-church pyramid" for Pentecost, plant a tree to celebrate the coming of spring, and help you pack a suitcase for summer vacation. Each message involves the children in a memorable experience that will help them relate the holiday to their Christian faith.

Active and meaningful children's messages require some planning. You'll need to gather the required supplies or props and you may need to recruit adult or teenage helpers. But the results will be worth the effort when you see children's faces light up as they find new meaning in special days.

5-Minute Messages for Children's Special Days includes major holidays such as Thanksgiving, Christmas, and Easter as well as lesser holidays including St. Francis Day, Columbus Day, and Presidents Day. Kids will also enjoy celebrating birthdays, adoptions, summer vacation, and even Super Bowl Sunday!

Not all the special days in this book conveniently fall on a Sunday or day of worship. That's OK. Use the messages in this book to help kids anticipate the special day. Build on kids' natural excitement by giving the corresponding children's message in the week prior to the day you'll be celebrating.

Before you give each message, talk with the children about the special day. Ask them to tell you what they look forward to most, what they remember from last year's observance, and what they hope will happen this year. Let them see that you, too, are excited about the special day ahead.

The messages in this book are meant to stimulate and invigorate your own creativity. Reading or memorizing them is out of the question! Put your own personality and creativity into the messages and enjoy the time you'll spend with God's little ones. May all your times with them be special days!

Part One:
Messages for Fall

1. Back to School

Note: *Check your local schools' schedules to find out when kids begin the new school year in your area.*

Theme: Beginning with God

Bible Text:
Praise the Lord, the God of Israel. He always was and always will be. Let all the people say, "Amen!" Praise the Lord! (Psalm 106:48).

Preparation: You'll need a pair of long pants, a sweater, a hat, gloves, and school supplies such as books, pencils, a backpack, a lunch box, and a bell. You'll also need one Bible-verse bookmark for each child.

The Message:

School starts this week! Let's think about how we might get ready for school. *(Choose a child to model school gear and clothes.)* Let's help dress this child for school before the bell rings. Hurry! We don't want to be late for school. *(Have kids hurry to dress the child. Periodically pretend you're going to ring the bell. Before children are finished, ring the bell.)*

(Have children respond to these questions.) What were you thinking as you dressed our student? What went through your mind when the bell rang and you weren't finished? How does it feel to be leaving the slow pace of summer and going to the faster pace of school?

Things will change when you go back to school. But one thing will stay the same. *(Read the Bible text.)*

No matter where you are—at home or at school; or how busy you are—God "always was and always will be." God is your oldest and closest friend. He was with you during the summer, and he will be with you when you go to school. You can talk to God in prayer any time you want—when you're in class, on the sports field, when you meet new friends, or begin to study a new subject.

(Hand out bookmarks.) Take this bookmark to school with you this week. Every time you look at the bookmark, remember that God is going to school with you. So let's celebrate that. When I say, "Let all the people say," you shout, "Amen! Praise the Lord!" *(Say, "Let all the people say," then cue children's response.)*

2. Where's Your Altar? (Labor Day)

Note: *Labor Day is the first Monday in September.*

Theme: Vocation

Bible Text:

Honor the Lord with your wealth and the firstfruits from all your crops (Proverbs 3:9).

Preparation:

You'll need a table; school supplies such as books, pencils, and paper; kitchen items such as pots, pans, and utensils; and a hammer. Set the school supplies, kitchen items, and hammer on the table.

Plan to give this message in your sanctuary or worship area. If your church doesn't have an altar, have children gather around a pulpit or podium. Tell your church pianist to be prepared to play "Praise God, from Whom All Blessings Flow."

As an additional feature of this message, you might encourage congregation members to bring items to church that best symbolize their professions or vocations.

The Message:

(Invite the children to the back of the church and ask congregation members to face the back.)

Labor Day is coming. Most of us think of Labor Day as the end of summer—families take their last weekend vacations, swimming pools close, and kids have to go back to school.

But Labor Day is more than just the end of summer vacation. Labor Day is a holiday that honors people who work. People all over the world work at different jobs every day. I have items here that people use in their work. When I hold them up, tell me what kind of work the people do. *(Hold up each item. As a child names the item and the occupation, give the item to the child.)*

Some people work to make money, some people work so they can help others, some people work so they can use their talents. These are all good reasons to work. But Christians have a really great reason to work. Let's read about it in the Bible. *(Read the Bible text.)*

Christians can praise and honor God with the work they do. In Bible times many people worked as farmers. They praised and honored God by giving God some of the crops they had raised. They would make a long parade and bring their gifts to God in the temple.

Today we can praise God in so many different ways. Let's bring our work before God as we remember Labor Day. Let's think of the many ways our work can be used to praise God. If we're students in school, how can we let our work praise God? *(Let the children respond.)* If we're helping mom or dad, how can our work praise God? *(Let the children respond.)*

Let's take our work items and bring them before God's altar. We'll have a long parade just like Israel did. If some of the moms or dads have work items with them, they might join us, too. We'll sing "Praise God, from Whom All Blessings Flow" as we march. Let's give our labor back to God on this Labor Day!

(Lead the children around the church, inviting the parents who have been alerted to bring their work tools with them to join you. Place the items on and around the altar as the hymn is being sung. Close in prayer, thanking God for all the workers in your church.)

3. God's Gossip
(Sunday School Opening Day)

Theme: The good news

Bible Text:
God loved the world so much that he gave his one and only Son so that whoever believes in him may not be lost, but have eternal life (John 3:16).

Preparation: You'll need a supermarket tabloid, a telephone, and a trash can.

The Message:

(Take out the tabloid and show it to the children.) Newspapers like this don't really print news; they print gossip or stories about people that may or may not be true. Supermarkets stock them near the checkout registers, and people buy and read them because the stories look so exciting. *(Read a headline.)* Do you think that's true? *(Let children respond.)* I don't think it's true. But people will read it and talk about it anyway.

Sometimes people share gossip on the phone. *(Pick up the telephone receiver.)* Hello (child's name). This is (your name). Did you hear that a dinosaur was spotted at (your church)? That's what I heard from (child's name). Can you imagine? A dinosaur in our church?

Some gossip is too outrageous to be believed. But I'm going to start some true gossip—some good gossip with (child's name). I want her to whisper whatever I tell her to the person next to her, and that person tell it to the person next to him, and so on all the way down the row and into the next row, until everyone has heard the news. While you're doing that, the congregation will softly sing a hymn.

(Start the congregation singing "I Love to Tell the Story" or another hymn about sharing the good news. Then whisper the Bible text to the first child and encourage her to whisper it to the person next to her. If children are confused, show them whom to whisper to next.)

Now let's hear what kind of gossip we have passed. We'll ask the last person to tell us what was whispered. *(Let the child deliver the message, which may or may not be the original verse.)*

What a great bit of gossip! *(Repeat the Bible text.)* Some gossip is not true—

that there's a dinosaur in our church, for example. But this gossip, this God-gossip, is absolutely true. Some gossip is not good to spread—especially if what we're saying is going to hurt other people. But God-gossip is great to spread! When people hear about God's love and believe in Jesus, then they're part of Jesus' family and will live with him forever.

In Sunday school we can hear God-gossip. We can invite our friends to come with us. We can let them know all about God's love, and they can tell others. That's how God-gossip gets spread—by one person telling another person how much Jesus loves us!

I don't think we need to read these gossipy newspapers. *(Put the tabloid in the trash can.)* And I know we don't need to use this telephone to spread gossipy stories. *(Hang up the telephone with a slam.)* But I do know we need to spread God-gossip. Let's all say it together. *(Repeat the Bible text with the children and the congregation.)*

4. Hooray for Our Team! (Football Season)

Note: *Football season usually begins the first weekend in September.*

Theme: Church support

Bible Text:
So encourage each other and give each other strength, just as you are doing now (1 Thessalonians 5:11).

Preparation: Collect football sports gear and clothing, such as helmets, pads, and jerseys.

The Message:

It's fall and that means it's time for football season! Football is an all-American sport, and many people in our country love to support their favorite teams. Let's see what teams you like to cheer for and why.

(Give children football gear and clothing to put on. Have children tell which football teams they like.)

When you go to a football game, it's almost as much fun to watch the fans as the football players. When your team scores a touchdown, what do you do? *(Let children respond.)*

Let's cheer for our teams right now! On the count of three, shout out the name of your favorite team. One, two, three! *(Pause for children to call out their teams. Then continue.)*

When fans want their team to stop the other team from scoring a touchdown, they often yell, "Defense! Defense!" Let's have all the people in our church try that on the count of three. One, two, three. *(Pause for people to shout, "Defense! Defense!" Then continue.)*

When fans want to show that they're rooting for their team, sometimes they'll do a "wave." Let's make a wave right now. *(Lead kids and the congregation in a coordinated wave.)*

Football games are so much fun. We're having fun together just thinking about football. Our church is kind of like a football team. We may not wear helmets or uniforms, but we're working together to tell people about Jesus. (Name of your pastor), our coach, encourages and leads us in the "game." Sometimes we win, and people come to know Jesus better. Sometimes we don't do so well. But we always need cheerleaders. Listen to what Paul said about cheering for your church. *(Read the Bible text.)*

There's one big difference between our church team and a football team—in the church the players are also the fans! We need to cheer for each other all the time.

Let's remember to cheer for our church! We do that by letting people know we appreciate what they do, by encouraging one another, and by praying for our church. Don't forget to cheer for your pastor, teachers, and other church workers. Here's a good cheer:

(Have all the children put one hand in the circle on top of yours. On the last "go," break the circle with kids raising their hands above their heads.)

Two, four, six, eight, who do we appreciate?

(Name of your church)! (Name of your church)!

Go, team, go!

5. A Blessing of the Animals (St. Francis Day)

Note: *The day of St. Francis is October 4.*

Theme: Creation

Bible Text:

So God made the wild animals, the tame animals, and all the small crawling animals to produce more of their own kind. God saw that this was good (Genesis 1:25).

Preparation: Use one of the settings suggested below or simply make this blessing part of your worship service.

● Invite children to bring their animals to the church on a given afternoon for an all-church pet show. Give children a chance to introduce and tell about their pets.

● Take a Saturday field trip to a nearby farm or zoo. Have children count all the different animals and birds they see.

● Set up a petting zoo in your church parking lot. Invite children to bring their pets and ask church or community members to bring small farm animals such as rabbits, sheep, or goats.

● Have a pet-wash for your church or community. Bring in lots of soap and washtubs and show your love for animals by bathing them.

● Have children draw pictures of their favorite animals and tell why they like that animal.

● Have children choose a favorite animal to imitate as a pianist plays an appropriate song, such as "All Creatures of Our God and King." You'll need photocopies of the "Prayer for the Blessing of the Animals."

The Message:

(Read the Bible text.) St. Francis of Assisi is known for his love of animals and all creation. He died October 3, 1226. Let's celebrate St. Francis Day with a prayer for the blessing of the animals.

Prayer for the Blessing of the Animals

PASTOR: Let us thank God for this wonderful world.

GIRLS: For the stars of the heavens, the sun and the moon,
the dark of the night, and the bright of the noon,

ALL: We thank you, Lord!

BOYS: For the rain that brings life, the wind in its motion,
the whispering snow, and the crash of the ocean,

ALL: We thank you, Lord!

MOTHERS AND DAUGHTERS: For corn and the grain of the wheat
so edible, for milk and cheese and fruit and vegetable,

FATHERS AND SONS: For meat that we eat, and the fish that are
net-able,

ALL: Incredible, Lord, incredible!

PASTOR: Now bless us, Lord, and bless please our animals.

DOG LOVERS: The dogs we bring whose happy barks
Remind us of Noah and the arfs on the ark.
Who chase after the Frisbee and fetch rubber balls,
Who love us with licking and come to our calls.
Bless poodles and cockers and shepherds and schnauzers,
Dachshunds and setters, bulldogs and Bowsers,
Of every kind and of proud pedigree;
And bless all the mutts with no family tree.
Keep them safe and healthy in this year to be.
For all our dogs, we thank you, Lord.
Bless them, Lord.
Amen.

CAT LOVERS: Bless all our cats, wise creatures of worth,
Who purr in our homes and prowl on our earth.
Bless cat and the kitten so soft in their stirring,
Who snuggle on our tummies, serenade us with purring.
Bless barn cats in the country and cats of the city,
Maltese, Siamese, and the common house kitty.
Keep safe from all danger, guard from all harm,
Protect as they wander, and bring safely home.
For all our cats, we thank you, Lord.
Bless them, Lord.
Amen.

PEOPLE WITH OTHER ANIMALS: For our fish in their swimming,
For birds on the perch,
For gerbils and hamsters and rabbits, of course.

17

Bless horses so noble and donkeys so humble,
Our sheep, pigs, and goats, and the hives of the bumble.
Bless snakes as they slither and mice in the pen.
ALL: Bless all of your creatures, Lord, again and again,
That we may love them as you love us all,
Given your grace—the great and the small.
Bless us we pray, in the Name of our Lord,
Amen and amen and amen!

6. A Columbus Day Trust Walk

Note: *Columbus Day is the second Monday in October.*

Theme: Discipleship

Bible Text:
Whoever serves me must follow me. Then my servant will be with me everywhere I am. My Father will honor anyone who serves me (John 12:26).

Preparation: You'll need a blindfold for each child and a few helpers to assist in putting on the blindfolds.

The Message:

This week we celebrate Columbus Day. It's a day we set aside to remember a great explorer. What's an explorer? *(Let children respond.)* Explorers go where other people have never been before. Do you think you'd like to be an explorer? *(Let children respond.)*

As much as I admire explorers, I also admire the people who follow explorers. They have to trust their leader. They have to go where their leader goes and do what their leader says to do.

Let's all get up and try an experiment. I'll choose (name a child) to be Christopher Columbus, and the rest of you will be the ship's crew. All of the ship's crew need to put on blindfolds. Some of my friends will help you tie them. While you're doing that, listen as I remind you of the story of Christopher Columbus. *(If it gets too noisy while the blindfolds are being put on, wait until everyone is done and then ask them to sit down for a moment.)*

In the year 1492, Christopher Columbus set out from Spain in search of a new world. In those days some people believed the world was flat. They thought if you kept on sailing you'd fall off the edge of the world. Now we know that's not true, but they didn't know that back then. Christopher Columbus believed that if you sailed long and far enough, you'd find new lands and could tell others about Jesus. So off he went! He was pretty brave to go where nobody had ever gone before.

All the children have their blindfolds on now so let's get in a line behind (leader's name), and we'll search for the new world. *(Help the children line up. Have the leader move slowly around. As you talk, help lead the blindfolded children.)*

They sailed and sailed for many days until they reached land. Christopher didn't really know where he was. He thought he was in the Indies so he called the

19

people Indians. He wasn't very kind to them, and we're sorry about that. But we still admire the good things he accomplished. Let's all go home now. *(Lead the children back to their seats and have them remove their blindfolds.)*

You were good followers. Let's give a hand to our explorers and our Christopher Columbus! How did it feel to follow an explorer? *(Let children respond.)* It's not easy to follow someone when you can't see where you're going. I'm sure Christopher Columbus' men felt that way, too. They didn't know where he was leading them!

As Christians, we're always following an explorer. Jesus is the greatest explorer of all. He leads us step by step through life. Listen to what he says about following him. *(Read the Bible text.)* Jesus wants us to follow him by serving others. When we follow Jesus, we're not sure where he'll lead us, but we know he'll always take care of us. He'll use us to tell others about him. We'll follow Jesus just as Christopher Columbus did! We, too, can be great explorers!

7. Masks (Halloween)

Note: *Halloween is October 31.*

Theme: Being honest

Bible Text:
You know when I sit down and when I get up. You know my thoughts before I think them (Psalm 139:2).

Preparation: You'll need a bag of candy or other treats and a collection of masks and costumes. Make a simple mask for each child and one for yourself. You can make simple masks out of paper bags, or staple 10-inch lengths of yarn to each side of a paper plate mask. Adult occupational clothing, such as police or firefighter hats or medical lab coats, makes great costumes for kids. Be sure to include Bible-times costumes if your church has them.

The Message:

Halloween is almost here! What an exciting holiday for kids! Long ago, people called Halloween "All Hallow's Eve." All Hallow's Eve was the day before All Saints Day when people would remember their friends and family members who had died and gone to live with Jesus in heaven. We don't take Halloween that seriously now. Now Halloween is a time to get dressed up in costumes and eat candy.

It's fun to dress up as someone else. I've brought some costumes like the ones you might wear on Halloween. *(Show children the costumes and help them put them on.)* Sometimes we wear masks with our costumes. *(Pass out masks to the children and keep one for yourself.)* It's fun to cover our faces and keep others from recognizing us. Let's cover our faces. Now let's uncover them.

But it's not fun to try to keep God from recognizing us. Sometimes people try to hide themselves from God like Adam and Eve did when they disobeyed God. When we pretend that the wrong things we do don't hurt God and others, that's like trying to hide from God. *(Hold your mask to your face. Have children hold up their masks, too. Then remove the masks and continue.)*

When we feel sad—but we don't want to talk to God about our sadness in prayer—that's like trying to hide from God. *(Hold your mask to your face and have kids hold up their masks, too. Remove the masks and continue.)*

When we get angry with others but we don't want to talk with them or ask

God to help us with our anger, that's like hiding from God and others. *(Hold your mask to your face and encourage children to do the same. Remove your mask and continue.)*

(Have children respond to these questions.) Can we hide from God? Why or why not? Even if you try to hide from God, can that keep God from loving you? Why or why not?

God knows who we are and loves us, even when we try to hide from him. There's no mask so good, no costume so wonderful, that can keep God from knowing who we are. Listen to what the Bible says about God knowing us. *(Read the Bible text.)*

God knows us and loves us—inside and out. On Halloween it's fun to disguise ourselves from other people, but we don't have to disguise ourselves from God. God knows us, and no matter who we are or what we've done, God loves us.

I have some trick or treat goodies for you. *(Pass out the treats you brought.)* This Halloween have fun disguising yourselves. But remember—you don't need to disguise yourself from God.

8. Boo! (Halloween)

Note: *Halloween is October 31.*

Theme: Don't be afraid

Bible Text:
Where God's love is, there is no fear, because God's perfect love drives out fear (1 John 4:18a).

Preparation: You'll need red construction paper and scissors. Before the message, cut out a red construction paper heart for each child. If you want, provide hearts for the adults in your congregation, too.

The Message:

(Invite the children to come forward, then let them gather in silence. When all are gathered, suddenly surprise them by saying loudly to the child nearest you . . .) BOO!

Did I scare you? Getting scared is part of the fun of Halloween, isn't it? When we want to scare someone, we say *(turn to another child and say loudly)* BOO!

So on Halloween it's fun to dress up in scary costumes or masks and go to parties or knock on doors for trick or treats. When people open the doors we can say *(turn to another child and say loudly)* BOO! and watch them jump. Scaring people on Halloween can be fun!

But there are times when it's not fun to be scared. Can you think of some times when it's not fun to be scared? *(Let children respond.)*

Some kids get scared when they're in bed at night, and it's very dark. Some kids worry about getting lost or having their moms or dads leave them.

And children aren't the only ones who get scared. Adults get scared, too. They worry about not having enough money to pay the bills, or they worry about losing their jobs, or lots of other things. Most of the time being scared isn't much fun.

(Pass out the hearts.) God doesn't want our hearts to be afraid, and he promises in the Bible that he'll be with us when we feel afraid. Listen to what the Bible says about being scared. *(Read the Bible text.)*

God's love for us is so perfect that we can count on God whenever we're afraid. We don't have to be afraid of the dark or of bullies or of being alone or not

23

having enough money or anything. We don't even have to be afraid of dying, because we know that when we die we'll go to heaven to be with Jesus.

On Halloween it's fun to scare each other. But this Halloween, remember God's love each time you say *(turn to a child near you and say loudly)* Boo! Because of God's love, we don't have to be afraid.

When I count to three, let's all throw our hearts up in the air and say, "We're not afraid!" together to help us remember God's love.

One, two, three: We're not afraid!

(Let children pick up their hearts before returning to their seats.)

9. We Are the Saints (All Saints Day)

Note: *All Saints Day is November 1.*

Theme: The church

Bible Text:

But you are a chosen people, royal priests, a holy nation, a people for God's own possession. You were chosen to tell about the wonderful acts of God, who called you out of darkness into his wonderful light (1 Peter 2:9).

Preparation: You'll need a large cardboard cross, pictures of saints or historic church figures, and pictures of yourself and other church members. Be sure to include pictures of several of the children you'll be talking to, but don't let them know. Your pictures of saints should include ancient saints such as St. Patrick and modern saints such as Mother Teresa. Affix double-sided tape to the back of each picture.

You'll also need name tags with the word "Saint" written on them. You can give them just to the children or to the whole congregation.

The Message:

Today is All Saints Day—a great day to remember all the saints of the church. Saints are people who love God, and many of them spend their whole lives serving him. On All Saints Day we especially remember people who loved God who are now in heaven. Can you think of some well-known saints who are now in heaven? *(Let children respond.)*

Two holidays we celebrate are named for saints—St. Valentine's Day and St. Patrick's Day. Today those holidays are mostly just for fun, but St. Valentine and St. Patrick were real people who loved Jesus and lived long ago. St. Patrick loved Jesus so much that he went around Ireland starting churches so people could hear about Jesus.

St. Patrick and St. Valentine are really famous saints. Let me show you pictures of some not-so-famous saints. *(Show pictures of saints or historic church figures. Explain who they are, then have children help you attach their pictures to the cardboard cross.)*

Not all saints lived long ago; there are many saints living and serving Jesus in our world today. Let me show you pictures of some recent saints. *(Show pictures of modern-day saints. Explain who they are, then have children help you attach their pictures to the cardboard cross.)*

As a matter of fact, you probably know a few saints. Let me show you pictures of some saints I know. *(Show pictures of yourself and other members of the congregation, then show pictures of children in your group. Have children help you identify each picture, then attach it to the cardboard cross.)*

That's right—you are saints! I am a saint. Anyone who loves and believes in Jesus is a saint. God made you a saint when he sent Jesus to die for you, and together we are the church, a great body of saints.

(Read the Bible text.) We can learn a lot about following Jesus from the saints who lived long ago and from the saints all around us today. But the best thing we can learn is that God made us saints through Jesus' death and resurrection. That's why we've put all these pictures of saints on the cross of their Lord. It's because of him that we are saints!

(Pass out the "Saint" name tags.) I've brought Saint name tags for us to wear today. When you get back to your seat, fill in your name next to the word "Saint." As we celebrate saints on this All Saints Day, we'll be celebrating you as well!

10. A Time to Vote (General Election Day)

Note: *General Election Day falls on the first Tuesday after the first Monday in November.*

Theme: Citizenship

Bible Text:

First, I tell you to pray for all people, asking God for what they need and being thankful to him. Pray for rulers and for all who have authority so that we can have quiet and peaceful lives full of worship and respect for God (1 Timothy 2:1-2).

Preparation: You'll need two baskets and two different kinds of candy (with enough pieces of each kind for every child). Give pre-printed campaign speeches to two children—one for each candy. For example, a campaign speech might say, "This is the best of all candies. It has both peanut butter and chocolate, melts in your mouth, and tastes great! People describe this candy as wonderful, fantastic, and good for you, too! So vote for this candy—and you'll be voting for the best."

The Message:

This coming Tuesday is a day of national election. That means that grown ups will have the chance to vote on people and make decisions about things that will influence our country's life for years to come. That's pretty exciting.

Who are some of the people we can choose to lead us? *(Let children respond.)*

In an election, people get to choose someone or something. Let's have an election here today. Ours is not nearly as exciting as the national election, but the choice is pretty important. I have two different candies here. I'll give out the candy that wins our election. *(Hold up two baskets of candy.)* Over here we have this candy *(describe its delicious features)* and over here we have this candy *(describe its delicious features)*. To help us in our election, we've asked someone to read a campaign speech for each candy. *(Have the campaign speeches read.)*

(Lead kids in voting. Then pass out the winning candy.) This is a silly election, isn't it? But in our national elections, the choices are very serious and that's why all adults are encouraged to vote on election days.

It's a wonderful blessing that we have in this land—to be able to choose our leaders and to make decisions about our future. Not everyone in the world can do that. In many lands, people are never able to vote in elections.

When you grow up, you'll be able to vote, too, and I hope you vote in each election. Think very carefully about the people you want to serve us, and vote with your head and heart.

Listen to what Paul says about our government. *(Read the Bible text.)* What does Paul tell us to do for our leaders? *(Let children respond.)* Even children can pray for our leaders, remembering that they serve God in serving us. Who would like to help us pray for our leaders right now? *(Invite the children to fold their hands. If a child is willing to pray, encourage him or her. Otherwise, pray for the coming election.)*

11. No Leftover Thanks! (Thanksgiving)

Note: *Thanksgiving is the fourth Thursday in November.*

Theme: Thanksgiving

Bible Text:
Always give thanks to God the Father for everything, in the name of our Lord Jesus Christ (Ephesians 5:20).

Preparation: No preparation is necessary.

The Message:

It will soon be Thanksgiving Day. That means people will gather together in church to give thanks to God for all they have. Many people will also gather at home around the table to eat turkey and other good things.

After the Thanksgiving meal, there will be lots of food left over. What do we call food that's left over? *(Let children respond.)* That's right! We call that food leftovers. We get leftovers after everyone has eaten the very best food first. I'm going to name some leftover foods. If you like that food, pop up where you're sitting and say "Yum! Yum!"

(Allow time between naming each food for children to pop up.) Turkey. Dressing/stuffing. Mashed potatoes. Cranberry sauce. Pecan pie. Hot rolls. Pumpkin pie. Mincemeat pie. Gravy.

What's the first thing you do on Thanksgiving Day? Watch a parade? Eat turkey? Get out of bed? *(Let children respond.)* God wants us to give him our first thoughts on Thanksgiving—and every day!

Yet we often give God our leftover thanksgiving. We thank our parents for working hard to earn money. We thank our friends for being our friends. We even thank the cook for cooking. Finally, we might get around to thanking God. But listen to what the Bible says about thanking God. *(Read the Bible text.)*

This Thanksgiving, how can we put God first? What's one thing you'd like to pop up and thank God for? *(Allow children to respond.)* Let's give God the best of our thanks and the best of our love on Thanksgiving Day and every day. No leftover thanksgiving for God. Give God the best!

12. Are You Ready for Winter? (Late Autumn)

Note: *This message is best given on a warm, late autumn day when winter is the last thing on anyone's mind!*

Theme: Being ready for Jesus' return

Bible Text:
So you also must be ready, because the Son of Man will come at a time you don't expect him (Matthew 24:44).

Preparation: You'll need winter clothing such as hats, gloves, coats, scarves, and boots. If you live in an area that gets snow or ice in the winter, you might also bring in snow shovels, tire chains, and ice scrapers.

The Message:

Winter's coming! I know that today the sun's shining and the weather's warm, but winter's coming! And that means months of cold weather, rain, or even snow. So I thought we'd better start getting ready. *(Start passing out winter clothing.)*

Here, (name of child), put on this hat. (Name of child), you'd better put a coat on so you don't catch cold. (Name of child), you'll need these gloves if you're going to carry a lunch box to school in this weather. *(Continue passing out clothing until you run out. If you brought snow shovels or other snow equipment, pass that out as well.)*

How does it feel to be dressed for winter? *(Let children respond.)* What would it be like to wear these things all day today? *(Let children respond.)*

Let's help each other get these hot winter clothes off! *(Help children remove the winter clothing.)*

How can you get ready for winter? *(Let children respond.)*

It's hard to get ready for winter while it's still autumn—especially when we have warm autumn days like today. But every year, I'm not ready for that first really cold day, and I have to run around the house looking for my winter clothes. But not this year! *(Hold up a hat and gloves.)* This year we're ready!

Jesus wants his followers to be ready for his coming as well. When he comes to take us to live with him in heaven, he doesn't want us surprised. Listen! *(Read the Bible text.)*

How can we get ready for Jesus' return? *(Let children respond.)*

It's hard to be ready for Jesus when our lives are going well, and we can't believe that tomorrow will be any different from today. But we know that someday our lives on this earth will end. That's one of the reasons we read God's Word and gather for worship and prayer—because we know that someday Jesus will come to meet us. We want to be ready!

And when Jesus comes for his church, we want to be ready, too!

13. No Time to Sleep (Hibernation)

Theme: Discipleship

Bible Text:
Think about Jesus' example. He held on while wicked people were doing evil things to him. So do not get tired and stop trying (Hebrews 12:3).

Preparation: You'll need a large blanket. Ask three congregation members to try to awaken the sleeping children with their needs. One might be a homeless person, the other a hungry person, and the third a lonely person.

The Message:

As winter approaches, some animals get ready to hibernate. What does it mean to hibernate? *(Let children respond.)* That's right—when the weather gets cold, bears, groundhogs, and other animals go into their caves or holes and sleep for the whole winter. Do you think you'd like to hibernate? *(Let children respond.)*

Let's see if we can hibernate. This big blanket will keep us warm in the winter! Animals don't use blankets, but let's cuddle underneath and see if we can fall asleep like the animals.

Now, we have to snore as loud as possible when we hibernate. People may try to wake us, but we're going to keep on sleeping no matter what. Ready? Let's snore!

(One by one, the three congregation members come to the "sleeping" group of children asking for their help. The homeless person might ask to come into the children's home, the hungry person might want food, and the lonely person might want a friend. Tell children to keep on sleeping and snoring. When all the interrupting people are gone, ask the children to come out from under the blanket.)

Did you hear anything when you were sleeping? What did you hear? *(Let children respond.)* I heard that, too. That reminds me of a Bible verse. *(Read the Bible text.)*

Sometimes we Christians get so tired of doing good that we want to hibernate and forget to help others. How do you think we could've helped those people? *(Let children respond.)* How has Jesus helped us? *(Let children respond.)*

Hibernation is good for bears, but the people of God need to stay wide-awake. Let's stay awake this winter.

Part Two:
Messages for Winter

14. As White as Snow (Winter)

Note: *The first day of winter is December 21.*

Theme: Forgiveness

Bible Text:
Though your sins are like scarlet, they can be as white as snow (Isaiah 1:18b).

Preparation:
You'll need scissors and a piece of white paper. You'll also need a white paper doily and a red construction paper slip for each child.

Before the service, practice cutting a paper snowflake. Fold a square piece of paper in half on the diagonal to form a triangle. Fold the paper two more times, forming a smaller triangle. Cut the unfolded edge in a curve. Cut several small triangles out of the folded edges and the edge you've trimmed. When you unfold the paper, you will have a snowflake shape.

If you live in a climate that gets snow, you may wish to bring in a bucket of fresh snow and make a snowball instead of a paper snowflake.

The Message:

Winter is here! In most places around the country, winter means snow! *(Begin to fold and cut the paper into a snowflake. Continue talking as you cut.)* A lot of people like snow. What can you do in the snow? *(Let children respond.)*

It's fun to walk in the snow. The snow crunches and your feet slide. Snow can be very beautiful to look at, too.

But a lot of people don't like snow. Why don't people like snow? *(Let children respond.)*

Let me read you a beautiful Bible verse about snow. *(Read the Bible text. Then give each child a red construction paper slip.)* Think about a sin you've done. Maybe you were angry with a friend or failed to be kind to someone. Maybe you disobeyed your parent. Let's pretend that your slip of paper is that sin.

The Bible says that God's forgiveness can make our scarlet sins as clean as snow. Lay your "sins" in a pile here on the floor.

Because God loves us, we can be as clean as freshly fallen snow. *(Open the cut*

34

paper to reveal the snowflake shape. Lay it on the pile of sins.)

What a great thing to remember when we see the snow. God forgives all our sins and covers us with his love. He sent Jesus into this world to die for us so that our sins would be taken away, and we can stand before him as pure as fresh snow.

(Give each child a paper doily. Have the children throw the doilies into the air and watch them flutter down.) The next time you see snow falling, remember that God makes you as pure as the snow because he forgives all your sins!

15. How to Be Really Ready (Advent)

Note: *Advent season begins the fourth Sunday before Christmas.*

Theme: Preparing for Christmas

Bible Text:

"Prepare the way for the Lord. Make the road straight for him." The people asked John, "Then what should we do?" John answered, "If you have two shirts, share with the person who does not have one. If you have food, share that also" (Luke 3:4b, 10-11).

Preparation: You'll need inexpensive Christmas cards and ornaments— enough so that each child can have one or the other. You'll need as many pens as you have cards. You'll also need a piece of Christmas candy, such as a candy cane, for each child.

The Message:

Christmas is only (number of weeks) weeks away, and it's time to get ready. *(Give cards and pens to some children.)* Why don't you kids start by signing these cards. *(Give ornaments to other children.)* You kids can decorate the front of the church here. *(Show Christmas candy.)* In a few minutes, I'll give you some Christmas candy.

What are some other ways to get ready for Christmas? *(Let the children respond.)*

When John the Baptizer came to help people get ready, he didn't have any Christmas decorations. And people didn't know anything about Christmas cards back then. John didn't eat Christmas candy; he ate locusts and wild honey. But he did have some great ideas about how to get ready for God's coming Savior. *(Read the Bible text.)*

Getting ready for Jesus means that we show his love to people. If people are hungry, we feed them. If people are cold or homeless, we help take care of them. That's what Jesus did for others—he showed great love for them. He even gave his life for us.

Jesus wants us to show love for those he loves—not only at Christmas, but all the time. And we can get ready for his coming by loving others right now!

Let's practice. Take one of the Christmas cards or decorations from the front of the church and give it to someone here in church. When you hand your gift to someone say, "Jesus loves you." *(Help each child get a card or ornament.)* And here's a piece of Christmas candy just for you! *(Give each child a piece of candy as he or she leaves the pulpit area.)*

16. The Last Christmas Present

Note: *This children's message works well either on Christmas Day (December 25) or during the week following Christmas Day.*

Theme: Christmas

Bible Text:

The Word became a human and lived among us. We saw his glory—the glory that belongs to the only Son of the Father—and he was full of grace and truth (John 1:14).

Preparation: You'll need four wrapped Christmas presents. Take one with you to the pulpit area. Before the service, give the other presents to three congregation members.

The Message:

Well, it's all over. Christmas has come and gone for another year. Tell me about some of your favorite Christmas presents. *(Let children respond.)*

But now it's all over. Pretty soon we'll be taking down the Christmas tree, putting away the decorations, and getting rid of all the wrapping paper. I think the saddest moment of Christmas is when you unwrap the last present. I've saved my last present to unwrap with you. Then it's all over.

(Unwrap the present. Let the kids see what it is.)

Well, that's it. No more presents. I guess Christmas is all over. Wait. I think there's one more gift in our church. Can you help me find it? *(Send kids out into the congregation to find the gifts. When the gifts are found, you're delighted! Take the first two, unwrap them, and show kids the presents. Don't open the last present.)*

You know, there really is never a last Christmas present. There's always one more. *(Read the Bible text.)*

When God gave us his Son for Christmas, God gave us a lifetime of gifts—our sins will always be forgiven, and the happiness we feel at Christmas is ours all year long. Even when we die we can go to be with God for a Christmas celebration that'll last forever.

There really is never a last Christmas present, is there? So I'm not going to unwrap this present. I'll set it right here as a reminder that there is no such thing as a "last" Christmas present!

17. What Do You Do With an Old Christmas Tree? (Sunday After Christmas)

Theme: After Christmas

Bible Text:

But when the right time came, God sent his Son who was born of a woman and lived under the law. God did this so he could buy freedom for those who were under the law and so we could become his children (Galatians 4:4-5).

Preparation: You'll need a Christmas tree with the decorations removed and about 2 feet of twine or rope.

Before the service, saw the top half off of the tree to create a smaller version of a Christmas tree. Next, saw the branches off the bottom half of the tree so that only the trunk remains. Cut the trunk almost through about one-third of the way down from the top.

The Message:

(Place the small undecorated tree before the children.)

What is this? *(Let the children respond.)* That's right—it's an old Christmas tree. An old, undecorated Christmas tree. It used to be so pretty standing in someone's living room with lights and presents around it. But now Christmas is all over, and it looks so sad.

Some people feel this way when Christmas is over—undecorated, dried up, and pretty sad. Christmas was so much fun for us, but with it all over, we just feel...well, undecorated!

But Christmas is just the beginning! At Christmas God sent his Son, Jesus, into the world to make us part of God's family forever. That part of Christmas is never over! Listen to what the Bible says. *(Read the Bible text.)* Jesus bought our freedom for us by dying on the cross. How can we make a cross out of this tree?

(Show kids how they can break the tree into two pieces by snapping the tree at the spot you've sawn through. Have kids help form a cross by binding the two pieces together with twine.)

How can our creation remind us of why Jesus came into the world for us? *(Let children respond.)* How can we make every day a Christmas Day this year? *(Let children respond.)*

We may be sad because Christmas Day is over for this year, but we know that it was only the beginning—the beginning of Jesus' life on earth and of our salvation.

(Save the cross to use in the children's messages for Ash Wednesday, "Time to Get Dirty" (p. 57) and for Good Friday, "My Cross" (p. 64).)

18. Measuring a Moment (New Year's Eve)

Note: *New Year's Eve is December 31.*

Theme: Time is in God's hands

Bible Text:
But I trust in you, O Lord; I say, "You are my God." My times are in your hands (Psalm 31:14-15a, NIV).

Preparation: You'll need two calendars—one from the old year and one from the new. You'll also need a kitchen timer or another timer with a loud alarm.

The Message:

Well, Christmas is past. What special things did you do over the Christmas holiday? *(Let the children respond.)*

There is still a very special day coming. It's New Year's Eve. What happens on New Year's Eve? *(Let children respond.)* That's right—we change years. As midnight on New Year's Eve approaches, we get ready to put away the old calendars *(put the old calendar behind you)* and get out the new *(hold up the new calendar)*.

We think about time on New Year's Eve. Is a year a long time? a month? a week? a day? How about a minute? Do you think a minute is a long time? *(Let children respond.)*

Let's find out. Turn to a person next to you. On "go," start talking to that person. You can talk about anything—about Christmas or school or a favorite hobby. But the two of you have to talk for one minute. I'll set the timer. Now, go! *(Let children talk for one minute. Then ring the alarm.)*

Now, we're going to be quiet for one minute. Not a word! Let's just sit in silence for one minute. Ready? Go! *(After 60 seconds, ring the alarm.)*

Was it harder to talk or be quiet for one minute? *(Let children respond.)* There are 525,600 minutes in a year. Every minute is a precious gift from God. Listen to what the Bible says. *(Read the Bible text.)*

All of our time is in God's hand. He's with us every minute of the day, every day and week and month and year. And he'll be with us forever and ever—for all of our time!

19. Time That Goes on Forever (New Year's Eve)

Theme: Time is a gift of God

Bible Text:
I will praise the Lord at all times; his praise is always on my lips (Psalm 34:1).

Preparation: None necessary.

The Message:

Christmas is past, and we've received some wonderful presents. Look what I got for Christmas. *(Hold up a present.)* What did you get for Christmas? *(Let children respond.)*

New Year's Eve is approaching and that tells us about other gifts from God. What gift of God do you think about on New Year's Eve? *(Let children respond.)*

A very important gift that God gives us is time. Time is made up of seconds and minutes, hours and days, weeks and months and years. Let's see how many months we have represented in this group today. On "go," get up and say your birth month over and over. If you were born in January, loudly say, "January, January" until others hear you. Take the hands of others born in your same month. Form groups according to the month you were born in.

(Help the children group themselves by birth months. You may want to fill in the absent months, or months where there might be only one or two children, with adults from the congregation.)

Now, let's take a count. Here is January. Here is February, March, April, May, June, July, August, September, October, November, and December. It looks like we have all the months represented. What do you think is special about your month? *(Let children and adults respond.)*

Each month is special in some way. What a wonderful gift time is. Listen to what the Bible says about time. *(Read the Bible text.)* The Bible says that all times give us the opportunity to praise God. This New Year's Eve, think of how you can praise God throughout the next year. Time is a such a special gift!

20. Megaphones (Epiphany)

Note: *Epiphany is January 6.*

Theme: Evangelism

Bible Text:

When Jesus was born, some wise men from the east came to Jerusalem. They asked, "Where is the baby who was born to be the king of the Jews? We saw his star in the east and have come to worship him" (Matthew 2:1-2).

Preparation: You'll need a megaphone (you can make one by taping paper into a cone shape) wrapped attractively in a large box. You'll also need a sheet of construction paper for each child and tape.

The Message:

Christmas is over, and January is upon us. We're in the season of Epiphany now. Christmas seems so far away. But look, I've found another present! *(Unwrap the box and take out the megaphone.)*

Do you know what this is? *(Let children respond.)* It's called a megaphone, and it's used to make someone's voice bigger so people can hear better.

While I tell you about megaphones and Epiphany, I'd like you to make a megaphone. It's easy. *(Demonstrate as you talk.)* You just roll a piece of paper into a cone and then tape it together. Some of our older kids can help you. *(Pass out paper and tape. Let the older children work with groups of two or three.)*

Listen to this Bible verse. *(Read the Bible text.)* The wise men wanted to find Jesus, but they didn't know where he was. So they asked. During the season of Epiphany, we celebrate that the wise men searched for and finally found Jesus.

A lot of people today don't know how to find Jesus. They forget that Christmas is all about Jesus. They don't know that Jesus is God's Son.

Are your megaphones ready? Hold them up when you get them done. We need to make our voices and our faith bigger so others will know about Jesus. Of course we can't yell at people, but how can we tell them about Jesus? *(Let children respond.)*

Let's gather around with our megaphones. I'm going to whisper a secret to you, and when I tell you, let all the congregation know the secret.

(Gather the children around. Whisper "Jesus was born for you!" Count "one, two, three," then turn and loudly share the message with the congregation through your megaphones!)

21. Follow That Star! (Epiphany)

Note: *Epiphany is January 6.*

Theme: Evangelism

Bible Text:
After the wise men heard the king, they left. The star that they had seen in the east went before them until it stopped above the place where the child was (Matthew 2:9).

Preparation: You'll need pictures of "stars" from newspapers or magazines. These stars could be from the worlds of sports, entertainment, politics, or religion. Have a large mirror hidden behind you as you talk to the children. You'll also need a stick-on star for each child.

The Message:

Epiphany is a fun word to say. Say that word with me: "e-PIF-a-nee!" On the day of Epiphany, we remember that a star once shone in the sky pointing the wise men to Jesus. *(Read the Bible text.)*

Today, when we talk about "stars" we don't always mean the bright lights in the sky. Sometimes we talk of famous people as being stars. I have pictures here, and I'd like to play a game with you. I'll hold up the picture, and if you know who the star is, raise your hand. Let's see who can identify the most stars. *(Play the game for a minute or two, calling on different children. Finally, hold up the large mirror in front of the children.)*

Now, who's the star? *(Let children respond.)* That's right—you are all stars when you point others to Jesus. That's what the Epiphany star did for the wise men. Whenever we show others Jesus' love and forgiveness, we're just like that Epiphany star.

(Give each child a stick-on star.) Put a sticker star on your shirt or dress. When someone asks you what that means, let them know that you are Jesus' Epiphany star!

22. Super Servants (Super Bowl Sunday)

Note: *The Super Bowl, a celebration of American football, occurs in late January.*

Theme: Servanthood

Bible Text:
Whoever wants to be the most important must be last of all and servant of all (Mark 9:35).

Preparation: You'll need squares of paper toweling, each with "#1" marked on them.

Well before the service, enlist the janitor or a helper to present this message with you. The helper should wear work clothes, push a vacuum cleaner, if possible, and carry a dust cloth. Have the helper carry the squares of paper toweling in a pocket, and show him or her where to find a pew Bible with a bookmark at the text. Make a photocopy of this message and have your helper memorize the "janitor" parts of the dialogue.

The Message:

Today is Super Bowl Sunday. Do you know who's playing today? *(Let the children respond.)* When the football game is over, one team and one city will hold up their fingers like this and say, "We're #1!" *(Point your forefinger upward.)* Let's all try that! *(Chant "We're #1!" with the children.)*

What a great afternoon this will be. The winner will really be #1 with lots of money and fame and power! *(At this point your helper will attract the children's attention by turning on the vacuum cleaner or whistling as he or she dusts.)*

You: What's that noise?

Janitor: I'm #1. I'm #1.

You: Why, it's *(say the helper's name)*, our janitor. What are you saying?

Janitor: I'm saying that I'm #1!

You: You can't be #1. You're not even playing in the Super Bowl today. How can you be #1?

Janitor: I'm #1 because I'm a servant. See—I clean your church, I dust your chairs, I make sure that your Sunday school rooms are ready to be used every Sunday.

You: But how does that make you #1? Only the winners are #1— like in the Super Bowl.

Janitor: No. That's the way everybody thinks, but Jesus tells us to think differently. Let me read you something from the Bible. *(The janitor takes the pre-marked Bible out of the pew and reads the Bible text.)*

You: Oh, I see. You mean that the greatest servant is #1.

Janitor: Yes, and since I'm the greatest servant in this group...

You: You're #1! I get it! The greatest servant is the greatest!

Janitor: Those guys playing football in the Super Bowl may fight hard and outthink one another and win a trophy and lots of money, but if you want to be #1 in Jesus' eyes, you serve harder—the way he came and served. Jesus even gave his life to save us. That's what makes him #1!

You: So if we want to be #1, I guess we'll have to work hard at serving others, too. How can we be #1?

Janitor: Well, I just happen to have some #1 dust rags here. If the kids took them to their seats and cleaned up around them, that would be a good start. Then they could put those dust rags in their pockets and carry them around all week to remind themselves that the one who is the greatest servant is the greatest of all— like Jesus our Lord, who was the greatest servant!

You: That would be the real "super" thing to do!

(Help the janitor distribute the dust rags.)

23. Seeing Shadows (Groundhog Day)

Note: *Groundhog Day is February 2.*

Theme: Patience

Bible Text:

But they who wait for the Lord shall renew their strength, they shall mount up with wings like eagles (Isaiah 40:31a, RSV).

Preparation: You'll need a strong flashlight. Darken the pulpit area if possible.

The Message:

This week a very strange event will occur in Punxsutawney, Pennsylvania. It's Groundhog Day, and people will gather to see if a certain groundhog will come out of his hole and see his shadow. Let me show you what will happen. You can all be groundhogs, and this flashlight will be the sun. *(Have the "groundhogs" get down on hands and knees.)* Lower your heads and look at the floor. When I shine the light on you, you can look up.

The story goes like this. *(Turn the flashlight on and shine the light on each child as you talk.)* If the sun is shining in Punxsutawney, Pennsylvania on Groundhog Day and the groundhog sees his shadow, that means there's six more weeks of winter. If the sun is not shining, the groundhog won't see his shadow, and spring should be just around the corner. *(Turn the flashlight off and have the children sit up again.)*

How easy or difficult was it to wait for the light to shine on you? *(Let children respond.)* How many of you are ready for winter to be over so you can play outside? *(Let children respond.)* Is it easy or difficult to wait for spring? Explain. *(Let children respond.)*

People look forward to Groundhog Day because they get very tired of winter by this time of the year. They want to start thinking about spring. It's always easier to look forward to something new when you know the old is going to end.

It's hard for us to wait for things.

The Bible has some good words for waiting. *(Read the Bible text.)*

47

What does it mean to "wait for the Lord"? *(Let children respond.)* We can have faith that God will bring good things to us when God is ready. Spring will come whether the groundhog sees his shadow or not. Your birthday will be here, and school will be out soon enough. Even though it's hard to wait, it's good to know that God will help us through all of our waiting time, making us strong, not like a groundhog, but like a mighty eagle.

Spring will come when God tells it to. You can count on God to send spring and all good things at just the right time.

24. Mixed-Up Love (Valentine's Day)

Note: *Valentine's Day is February 14.*

Theme: God's love

Bible Text:
But God shows his great love for us in this way: Christ died for us while we were still sinners (Romans 5:8).

Preparation: You'll need four large tagboard signs, preferably in red, with the letters L, O, V, and E printed on them. As the children come forward, choose four kids to hold the signs. The signs should be facing their bodies initially. Position the children so that the letters are out of order. You'll also need a set of five signs with the letters J, E, S, U, S printed on them. You can give candy hearts to the children if you wish.

The Message:

Pretty soon it will be Valentine's Day. Valentine's Day is about love. To help us remember, I've asked some of our friends to help us keep love in plain sight. Turn the signs around, kids! *(When the children turn the signs, the letters will be out of order.)*

E-O-V-L. That's crazy! What's "eovl"? Is that a new rock group? It seems a little mixed up. *(Have children shout out what's wrong with the signs.)* Let's turn the signs over again and move around a bit. *(Move the kids around so that the letters are still out of order.)* Now turn the signs around.

V-E-O-L? That's sounds like a musical instrument! *(Have children shout out what's wrong with the signs again.)* It's all mixed up again! Oh, I'm so sorry. We'll try again. Let's hide your signs. *(Rearrange the children so that the letters are still out of order.)*

O-V-E-L. Isn't that a shape? Now it's really mixed up. Maybe you kids could help. How shall we arrange these letters to tell us what Valentine's Day is all about? *(Let the kids reposition the four children with their signs to spell L-O-V-E.)*

That's right! Let's give ourselves a big hand! It's really hard to get "love" right, isn't it?

It seems like a lot of people have a hard time getting love right. There's so much fighting and hatred in our world. It's not hard spelling love, but it's really hard doing love.

That's why God decided to love us in a special way. *(Pass out the new signs to different children, making sure that the letters are in the correct order.)* Now let's see how God spells love. *(Turn the J-E-S-U-S signs around.)*

On Valentine's Day when we remember love, let's remember Jesus, who is God's valentine to us. *(Read the Bible text.)*

Sometimes we can get love all mixed up. We need to remember Jesus, who taught us how to love the way God wants us to. Jesus is God's special valentine!

(Pass out candy hearts.)

25. A Valentine to God (Valentine's Day)

Note: *Valentine's Day is February 14.*

Theme: Showing love

Bible Text:
And God gave us this command: Those who love God must also love their brothers and sisters (1 John 4:21).

Preparation: You'll need a big envelope with the word "God" written on it and two valentines for each child—an inexpensive kids' assortment will do.

The Message:

Valentine's Day is coming. What do you do to celebrate Valentine's Day? *(Let the children respond.)* On this day of the year, we take time to tell people how much we love them. I have some cards here that do that. *(Read some of the cards. Then give each child two valentines.)*

Who are some of the people you'll send valentines to? *(Let the children respond.)* Now, take one of your valentine cards and give it to someone here in our church. *(Allow kids time to return. When everyone has come back, hold up the envelope with the word "God" written on it.)* It's hard to get God's address, but by showing love to God's people with your valentines just now, you gave a valentine to God. Let's hear what God has to say about what he would like for Valentine's Day. *(Read the Bible text.)*

We are valentines to God! God wants us to be living valentines for him. *(Have children respond to these questions.)* How can we show love to others in our family? at school? in our neighborhoods? When we tell other people about Jesus or feed the hungry or visit the lonely or help the homeless, we're loving the way God wants us to love. And that makes us God's valentines.

Keep a valentine to remind you that you are a valentine to God.

26. Real Leaders (Presidents Day)

Note: *Presidents Day is the third Monday in February.*

Theme: Leading by serving

Bible Text:

All of you must yield to the government rulers. No one rules unless God has given him the power to rule, and no one rules now without that power from God (Romans 13:1).

Preparation: You'll need large pictures of George Washington and Abraham Lincoln. (Your local library can probably lend you a book with good illustrations.) You'll also need one penny for each child.

Before the service, ask two or more children to usher the other children to the pulpit area for the message. Show your ushers how to stand by each row of seats in the sanctuary and motion the children forward.

The Message:

It's now time for our children's message. I've asked (name the children who will be acting as ushers) to help usher the children forward. Wait until the usher stands by your row and motions you forward before you come to the pulpit area.

(After all the children have been seated in the pulpit area, begin your message.)

Next Monday is Presidents Day. What is Presidents Day? *(Let the children respond.)*

It's a nice holiday. Most of you will get out of school for a day, and some of your parents even get the day off from work. But Presidents Day is also important because it allows us to remember two very great men—George Washington and Abraham Lincoln.

What do you remember about George Washington? *(Let the children respond.)* He is called the Father of Our Country. He was our first president and a man who led our nation both as a soldier and as president.

What do you know about Abraham Lincoln? *(Let the children respond.)* Abraham Lincoln was our 16th president. He was called the Great Emancipator because he led the fight to set black people free from slavery. Emancipate means to set free.

Both George Washington and Abraham Lincoln were great leaders of our country, but they also were servants—they put other people before themselves. It's like when (name the children who acted as ushers) ushered you to your seats this morning. They were leaders, but they let you go first.

(Ask the ushers these questions.) How did it feel to lead other children today? How did it feel to have to let people go before you? *(Ask the other children this question.)* How did it feel to follow our leaders?

When our leaders forget to think of others first, our nation can have some terrible troubles. But when our leaders lead by serving, we can be grateful to God for them.

Let me read to you what the Bible says about our leaders. *(Read the Bible text.)* We thank God today for two of our national leaders—George Washington and Abraham Lincoln. They were both great leaders and great servants. We can all lead by thinking about what's good for God and others before we think about what's good for ourselves. What are some ways we can do that? *(Let children respond.)*

I'm going to give each of you a picture of Abraham Lincoln that you can carry around with you all the time—it's on a penny. *(Give each child a penny.)* I'd give you a picture of George Washington, but he's on a dollar, and I don't have enough money!

Remember as you carry Lincoln's picture with you that God wants us all to lead by doing what's good for others.

Part Three:
Messages for Spring

27. Springing Up (Spring)

Note: *The first day of spring falls in late March on the day of the vernal equinox.*

Theme: New life

Bible Text:
Look at the new thing I am going to do. It is already happening. Don't you see it? I will make a road in the desert and rivers in the dry land (Isaiah 43:19).

Preparation: None necessary.

The Message:

It's spring!

How do you know it's spring? *(Let the children respond.)* There are signs all around us if we look. The birds are singing, the weather is warmer, there are buds on the trees. Everything is springing up from the earth. To spring means to jump out. Try a little springing with me. *(Lead the children in short spurts of jumping.)*

Right now, seeds that were planted deep in the earth last fall are beginning to grow. Pretty soon you'll see little green shoots come up. Then plants and flowers will appear. That's the beauty of spring. Out of the cold, hard, winter ground comes new life.

Let's pretend to be seeds deep inside the earth. *(Have children sit on the floor, wrap their arms around their knees, and tuck in their heads. Read the Bible text.)*

Our God loves life! He gave each of us our life. But he didn't stop there—he gives us new life over and over again every day. Each time we make right choices to love and be kind, we grow inside. That's new life. Raise your arms to sprout out of the earth. God sent his Son into the world to give us all the life we'll ever need. "I have come that they might have life," Jesus said. Come up on your knees and bask in God's warm love through his Son.

When we sin against God, we begin to wilt. Let your arms fall. But God's forgiveness in Jesus lifts us up. That makes us happy. God forgives us and we keep growing. That good feeling inside when we're forgiven is new life! Stand up and reach toward God's Son. Just like the earth is bursting with new life each spring, God gives us new life inside over and over again.

Spring is a time to see new life. Look for it around you. But don't forget to look for it in yourself.

28. Rain Gear (Rainy Days)

Theme: Joy

Bible Text:
Be full of joy in the Lord always. I will say again, be full of joy (Philippians 4:4).

Preparation: You'll need an umbrella with a "Be full of joy in the Lord always!" sign taped underneath it.

The Message:

Oh, the rain! It's been raining for so long! I guess that's good. We need rain. Why do we need rain? *(Let children respond.)* Rain is good for lots of things. We need it for the farmers' fields and to fill the reservoirs and lakes. But we need to be prepared when we go out in the rain, don't we?

Sometimes it feels like sad things are raining down on us. What are things that make you sad? *(As children respond, write each thing on a separate sheet of paper.)*

We need to be prepared to keep from being discouraged or depressed. *(Open the umbrella and give it to the children.)* Use this umbrella to keep those sad things away. *(Have kids try to hide behind the umbrella. Read each paper, wad it up, and then throw it at the kids. Hit the umbrella sometimes and hit unprotected kids sometimes.)*

How did the umbrella protect you from these sad things? *(Let children respond. Then read the sign under the umbrella.)* How does God's joy protect us from being sad? *(Let children respond.)*

(Read the Bible text.) Just as this umbrella keeps the rain from soaking us, God's joy keeps us from being depressed and discouraged.

29. Time to Get Dirty (Ash Wednesday)

Note: *Ash Wednesday falls 40 days before Easter (not including Sundays), usually in late February or early March.*

Theme: Repentance

Bible Text:
I become like dirt and ashes (Job 30:19b).

Preparation: You'll need a bowl of ashes and a wet, soapy washcloth. Church-supply stores often carry packaged ashes during the Lenten season. You'll also need a wooden cross. (You may want to use the cross you saved from the "What Do You Do With an Old Christmas Tree?" message on page 39 or make a new one out of two wood planks.)

The Message:

This is the time of year when people actually want to get dirty!

Most of the time our parents tell us not to get dirty. They want us to wash our hands and faces. But not now! It's the beginning of Lent. I'll explain what I mean about getting dirty in a moment.

(Show children the cross.) Lent is the time when Christians in many churches think about the suffering and death of Jesus. It reminds us of how much Jesus loved us and how our sins put him on a cross like this one. Lent lasts for 40 days, and then we celebrate the happy time of Easter. *(Put the cross away.)*

A long time ago when people were sad over their sins they would put ashes on themselves. I'm going to put some ashes on you to show you what I mean. *(As you talk, mark yourself, and then each child, with a cross-shaped smudge of ash on the forehead.)* They would get dirty on the OUTSIDE to remind themselves and others of the sin on the INSIDE. When poor old Job in the Bible felt bad about his sin, this is what he said: *(Read the Bible text)*. His wrongdoing made him feel dirty! On Ash Wednesday many people still go to church. They have their pastors put a little bit of ash on them as a reminder of their sins, as we're doing now.

God doesn't need the ashes on our foreheads to tell him how dirty we are. He already knows it! But when God looks at us, he sees us with eyes of love. And he doesn't want us to stay dirty. He sent his Son to die for us so that we could be clean again. *(Take the washcloth and wipe their foreheads clean.)* It doesn't matter how we sin. If we come to God, confess our sins, and are sorry, he makes us clean again. Jesus' death takes away that sin. We need to remember that we are "dirty" sinners. But even more, we need to remind ourselves that God has made us clean saints and children!

Ash Wednesday may be the time to get dirty. But as you wait for Easter to come, remember that God loves you. He makes you clean forever!

30. Shamrock Stories (St. Patrick's Day)

Note: *St. Patrick's Day is March 17.*

Theme: Faith of the saints

Bible Text:
So go and make followers of all people in the world. Baptize them in the name of the Father and the Son and the Holy Spirit (Matthew 28:19).

Preparation: You'll need shamrock stickers to give the children at the end of the message.

The Message:

Why are people so happy on St. Patrick's Day? *(Let children respond.)*

People celebrate with parties, they wear green, and sing old songs. Why? *(Let children respond.)* Maybe it's because March is one of those months without a holiday in it. It gives people a reason for a party.

In Ireland, St. Patrick's Day isn't celebrated the way it is here. The people there go to church on St. Patrick's Day to give thanks for a very great man. His name was Patrick and he lived around the year 400.

Patrick was an Englishman. He was kidnapped when he was a child and taken to Ireland to work as a slave. He grew to love the Irish people. Later Patrick became a church leader. His greatest wish was to tell the Irish people about Jesus. One of the best things you can do for someone you love is to tell them about Jesus. That's what Jesus meant when he said this to his disciples: *(read the Bible text).*

(Hold up a shamrock sticker.) Have you ever seen one of these before? It's called a shamrock. St. Patrick used the shamrock to teach people about God. There is one God *(point to the shamrock),* but three persons in one: God the Father, Son, and Holy Spirit. *(Point to each leaf of the shamrock.)*

Take a shamrock and go to someone in our congregation. Tap that person with the shamrock and say, "Jesus loves you!" Afterward, keep your shamrock and let it remind you to tell others about God the Father, the Son, and the Holy Spirit. *(Give each child a shamrock and send kids on their mission.)*

31. Fools for Christ (April Fools' Day)

Note: *April Fools' Day is April 1.*

Theme: Being wise in God's eyes

Bible Text:

Do not fool yourselves. If you think you are wise in this world, you should become a fool so that you can become truly wise, because the wisdom of this world is foolishness with God (1 Corinthians 3:18-19a).

Preparation: Before the service, make a dunce cap rolled from construction paper for each child, if possible. Write the words "Fool for Christ" on the side of each rolled cap. One dunce cap should have only the word "Fool" written on it.

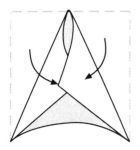

Fold in top corners on a large piece of construction paper.

Overlap and tape in place.

Trim bottom for a more finished look.

The Message:

It's almost April Fools' Day—April 1. I'd like to talk with you about "fools."

A long time ago when teachers wanted to correct a student for making a mistake or for doing something wrong, they would do a terrible thing. They'd sit the child on a stool in front of all the other kids. Then they'd put this silly cap on the child's head. *(Show the rolled dunce cap with "Fool" printed on it.)*

60

Once the cap was on, they'd make fun of that person. They wanted the child to look and feel foolish. They thought if the child felt really embarrassed he or she would never make that mistake or do that wrong thing again.

Do you think making a child look and feel foolish is a good way to discipline? *(Let children respond.)* When we make someone look foolish, we make them feel bad, and that's not kind, is it? A fool is someone who doesn't look good in other people's eyes. No one likes to be thought of as a fool.

But there is another kind of fool—one the Bible says we SHOULD become. St. Paul says that people will hear what Christians say about God, and it will sound very foolish to them. In their eyes we will be "fools for Christ." Listen to what he wrote. *(Read the Bible text.)*

If I were to tell someone that Jesus loves them, it might sound very foolish to them. They might think I was a fool. *(Put a dunce cap with "Fool for Christ" on yourself.)* If (name of child) were to tell another person that God forgives them for sinning, they might think, "That's dumb!" And (name of child) would be thought of as a fool. *(Put a "Fool for Christ" dunce cap on the child.)*

If (name of child) were to make friends with someone that nobody else liked because she knew Jesus wanted her to, others might make fun of her. They'd think of her as a fool. *(Put a "Fool for Christ" dunce cap on that child's head.)*

Now it's not really so bad being an April fool when we do what God wants us to do! We please him, even though others think we're foolish. And pleasing God is the best thing of all. *(Form pairs. Have kids each tell one good way they can be a "Fool for Christ" this April Fools' Day. Then have the other child put the "Fool for Christ" hat on the child.)*

This April Fools' Day think of a good way you can be a "Fool for Christ." Do something that God wants you to do, no matter how much others might think you're an April fool!

(Pass out the remainder of the dunce caps.)

61

32. Raise Those Palms (Palm Sunday)

Note: *Palm Sunday is one week before Easter Sunday.*

Theme: Praise

Bible Text:

Many people spread their coats on the road. Others cut branches from the trees and spread them on the road (Matthew 21:8).

Preparation: If palms are used on Palm Sunday in your church, have them brought forward for the children's message. If not, a simple palm branch can be used to illustrate the talk.

The Message:

This is Palm Sunday. Does anyone know why it's called Palm Sunday? *(Let the children respond.)* One day, many hundreds of years ago, Jesus was preparing to go to the city of Jerusalem to die. He entered Jerusalem in a very simple way, sitting on a peaceful little donkey. The people of Jerusalem were so happy to see him that they had a great parade to welcome him. Listen to what the Bible says about that day. *(Read the Bible text.)*

It must have been a great parade for our Lord! People were shouting "hosanna!"; that means "Come and save us, Lord!" The branches they cut off the palm trees were palm branches. Today many people in churches around the world bring in palm branches to remind them of the praise that was given to Jesus when he first entered Jerusalem.

That's why today is called Palm Sunday.

There's another kind of palm. Everybody has a palm somewhere on their body. Can you point to your palm? *(Let the children respond.)* That's right, it's in the center of your hand. We call it the palm of your hand! When we're excited and happy, we raise our hands to cheer and yell! Try it with me. Raise your hands and cheer. *(Let the children respond.)*

We don't need special branches to welcome Jesus on Palm Sunday. We can all raise our hands—our palms to welcome Jesus into our lives. The crowds in Jerusalem shouted, "Hosanna! Blessed is he who comes in the name of the Lord!"

Let's raise our palms and say that. *(Lead the children in raising their hands and shouting. Invite the congregation to join you.)*

There is another way to praise Jesus with our palms. That's by serving and helping other people. When we help people we are praising Jesus with our palms as well. That's what lending a helping hand means. If I lift you up when you are weak *(lift up a child)*, I'm using my hands, my palms, to help you. When I pat you on the back *(pat child's back)*, my palm is being used to love you and encourage you. That's praising Jesus. If I give you a handshake, that's showing encouragement, too. Let's all do that now. *(Have kids go into the congregation and congratulate all ages for reaching out.)*

It's nice to have palm branches in church on Palm Sunday, but the palms we carry on our bodies can always be used to help God's people and bring praise to Jesus. We don't have to wait for a special occasion. Let's raise our palms one more time in praise of the coming King. We'll say, "Hosanna! Blessed is he who comes in the name of the Lord!"

One, two, three. *(Raise palms and shout together. Again, encourage the congregation to join you.)*

33. My Cross (Good Friday)

Note: *Good Friday is the Friday before Easter Sunday. When used during a worship service, this message is effective for both children and the congregation as a whole. However, to avoid frightening the children, don't dwell on the gruesome details of crucifixion.*

Theme: Redemption

Bible Text:
But God shows his great love for us in this way: Christ died for us while we were still sinners (Romans 5:8).

Preparation: Before the service, make a large cross out of two pieces of wood. Any size lumber will work, but the bigger and more realistic the cross is, the more effective it will be. (You might consider using the cross you saved from the "What Do You Do With an Old Christmas Tree?" message on page 39).

You'll also need several hammers and small nails, as well as helpers to assist the children. Choose a song about repentance to sing at the conclusion of the message.

The Message:

(Gather the children on the floor around the cross.)

Pretty soon it will be Good Friday. That's a very strange name for a very awful day. What happened on Good Friday? *(Let the children respond.)* Jesus died on the cross for us on that Friday, long ago. Dying on a cross is called crucifixion. While it was awful for Jesus, it was good for us. He died and took away our sins so that we could be with God forever and ever.

To be crucified means to be nailed to a cross. It was a terrible way to die. Jesus must have loved us very much to allow himself to be killed that way.

Listen to what St. Paul says about Jesus' crucifixion. *(Read the Bible text.)* God put all of our sins on Jesus and nailed them to the cross with his Son. He did that so we would never again be far away from God.

One way to remember that is to take a nail and pound it into this cross we have here. As I pound the nail in *(hammer a nail)*, I remember that Jesus took all of my sins with him to the cross. I will never again be far away from God because of my sins.

Good Friday was not so good for Jesus, but it was very good for us. To help you remember what Jesus did for you, each of you will have a chance to take a nail and carefully pound it into the cross. While you hammer the nail, think about Jesus taking all of your sins to the cross. I've asked some of my friends to come and help us. Our congregation will sing a hymn as we remember Jesus' love for us.

(Have the congregation sing an appropriate song about repentance as the helpers assist the children in hammering nails into the cross.)

34. A Meal to Remember (Passover)

Note: *Passover begins on the evening of the Friday before Easter.*

Theme: God's deliverance

Bible Text:
You must celebrate the Feast of Unleavened Bread, because on this very day I brought your divisions of people out of Egypt. So all of your descendants must celebrate this day. This is a law that will last from now on (Exodus 12:17).

Preparation: You'll need a few items used in Passover meals such as matzo (unleavened bread available in most grocery stores), horseradish, parsley, and grape juice. Have the foods on a small table near you, along with plates, cups, and utensils for children to use. You might also want to recruit helpers to serve the food to children as you deliver the message.

The Message:

This is the time of year when our Jewish friends are observing Passover. How many of you have ever been to a Passover meal? *(Let the children respond.)* Passover is a very special time for Jewish families. In the Old Testament, God commanded his people to celebrate the Passover. It was to remind them that God delivered Israel out of slavery in Egypt. Listen to what God says to the Jewish people in the book of Exodus. *(Read the Bible text.)*

I've brought some foods today that are used in a Passover meal. I'll explain them to you. You can take a little taste of each as I tell you about them. *(Pass the foods around as you talk about each one.)*

MATZO is a special kind of bread. It's different than our bread because it doesn't have any yeast in it. Yeast, or leaven, makes bread rise up light and fluffy. The Jewish people were in such a hurry when they left Egypt that they used unleavened bread. That's bread without yeast in it. They had to leave so fast they couldn't wait around for their bread dough to rise. So Passover came to have another name—the Feast of Unleavened Bread. When we taste the unleavened bread, we remember how quickly the Jews had to leave Egypt.

HORSERADISH is so hot it can make us cry. Put a little bit on the unleavened bread and taste it. The Jewish people say that when tears come to their eyes, they weep for those in captivity. They remember how God brought them out of slavery. He brought an end to their tears.

PARSLEY is a sign of spring. It tastes fresh. It also reminds us that God's freedom is always fresh and growing.

WINE is served at Passover meals, too. We'll use grape juice today. Wine was a very common drink in Old Testament times. It reminds us of gladness and celebration. We're glad that God gives freedom to his people!

I didn't bring the main course for the Passover meal today. It's roasted lamb. Lamb is used for a special reason. While the Israelites were slaves, God told Pharaoh to let them go. But Pharaoh wouldn't listen. Finally, God sent an angel of death to convince Pharaoh to let the Israelites go. All who had blood from a lamb over their doorways would be kept safe or "passed over" by the angel of death. Only the Israelites obeyed. Pharaoh knew God was real when the Israelites were not hurt by the angel of death. He told them to leave Egypt. They were no longer his slaves.

The Passover meal is a way of remembering the mighty things God did for Israel. Jesus was celebrating Passover with his disciples on the night when Judas betrayed him. He told them to remember him when they broke the bread and shared the Passover cup of wine. As Christians, we do that when we celebrate Holy Communion in our churches.

Let's never forget that God delivers his people. He saved the Israelites at the time of the first Passover. He saves us now through the death of his Son, Jesus. Let's remember Jesus at this Passover time of year!

35. Where's the Alleluia? (Easter Sunday)

Note: *Easter Sunday is the first Sunday following the first full moon on or after the vernal equinox—always between March 22 and April 25.*

Theme: Joy

Bible Text:

He showed them his hands and his side. The followers were thrilled when they saw the Lord (John 20:20b).

Preparation: Make a large, brightly colored banner with the word "Alleluia!"

sewn or glued on it. At the beginning of Lent, have a ceremony in which a group of children carry the banner from the church sanctuary. The banner may then be hidden for the 40 days prior to Easter. It should be explained that Lent is a sad time and no "alleluias" will be sung.

If hiding the alleluia banner at Lent is not possible or desirable, the banner may be hidden on Easter morning within the worship space. Have an Easter hymn ready for the congregation to sing.

The Message:

Happy Easter to you! Christ is risen! He is risen indeed! On Easter we celebrate Jesus' resurrection from the dead. Because he rose from the dead, we will rise one day, too. That makes us very happy. When Christians are happy, they say the Easter word "alleluia!" It means "Praise the Lord!"

At first, Jesus' friends were not happy on Easter morning. They were sad because he was dead. Mary Magdalene was crying outside the tomb where they had buried him. She had come to check on his body. When she got there, Jesus' body was gone! She didn't know where he was.

But then Jesus appeared to her. She was so happy! She went to tell the disciples. They all rejoiced together! Listen to what the Bible says. *(Read the Bible text.)* When you see the Lord, you're filled with joy. You want to shout "alleluia!"

Sometimes our alleluias are hard to find. There can be things in our life that make us sad or unhappy. We don't feel like saying "alleluia!" So our alleluias seem to be hidden and silent. Then we've got to search hard to find one!

Somewhere in this room there is a banner hidden with the word "Alleluia!" written on it. While the congregation sings the next song, I'd like you to search around us for the alleluia banner. It could be in a corner, under a chair, in a pew, or up on a shelf. It's here somewhere! When you find it, let everyone know by shouting "alleluia!"

(While the children search for the banner, have the congregation sing. When the banner is found, lead the children in chanting "alleluia!" Have them bring the banner to the front where it can be unrolled and hung up.)

Easter is the time to sing and shout "alleluia!" We can do that even if our alleluias seem to be hidden. May this be a joyful "alleluia!" day for you.

36. A Lamp to Our Feet (National Library Week)

Note: *Each year a week in mid-April is designated as National Library Week. Call your local public library to get exact dates. The observance provides a good occasion to encourage not only reading in general, but reading of the Scriptures in particular. This message is also suitable for Bible society observances.*

Theme: Reading

Bible Text:
Your word is like a lamp for my feet and a light for my path (Psalm 119:105).

Preparation: You'll need a piece of paper with the word "cat" written on it, and various kinds of books such as dictionaries, encyclopedias, children's books, cookbooks, and a Bible. If possible, have Bibles for children to take home.

The Message:

One of the best gifts God has given us is the ability to read. How many of you know how to read? *(Let children respond.)* Pretty soon all of you will know how to read. In school, you learn your ABCs first. Then you learn simple words like *(hold up the piece of paper with the word "cat" printed on it).* Then you learn whole sentences, then paragraphs, then you're reading pages. Pretty soon you can read a whole book! What a wonderful thing it is to read your first book!

There is so much to learn about our world. These encyclopedias and dictionaries have information telling all about God's creation. Let's have (name of an older child who reads well) open this encyclopedia and read us something. *(Have the child open an encyclopedia to any page and read a few sentences.)* Now we know something that we didn't know before!

Other books are very practical. This cookbook tells us how to make spaghetti. Let's ask (name of another older child) to read how to make the sauce. *(Have the child read directions for spaghetti sauce from a cookbook).* Yum! I'm hungry!

There are some books we read just for fun. Here's a storybook about *(describe subject).* I'll bet that would be a fun book to read. The Bible is a very special kind of book. Let's see what it says. I'll ask (name of older child) to read a sentence from Psalm 119. *(Have Psalm 119:105 marked and have the child read the Bible text.)*

Why do you think God says the Bible is like a light? *(Let children respond.)* What does a light do? *(Let children respond.)* How is that like the Bible? *(Let children respond.)* How does the light of the Bible show us right from wrong? *(Let children respond.)*

It's great to be able to read about God in the Bible.

It's also great to be able to read about God and his world in all these books. This coming week is National Library Week—a time to visit our library and get some good books to read. It's also a good time to remember to read the Bible—the lamp for our feet and the light for our path.

(If you have Bibles, pass them out for children to take home.)

37. Time to Plant (Arbor Day)

Note: *Check with your local library for the date your community celebrates Arbor Day.*

Theme: God provides

Bible Text:
Let the fields and everything in them rejoice. Then all the trees of the forest will sing for joy before the Lord, because he is coming. (Psalm 96:12-13a).

Preparation: You'll need to purchase a healthy young tree. Before the service, have a hole for the tree dug and watered. Enlist the aid of other adults to help plant it after the children's message. Involve the children in placing the sapling into the ground and shoveling the dirt on top of it.

The Message:

An important holiday is coming, though it isn't as well known as Christmas or Easter. It's called Arbor Day. It's a day set aside for planting trees.

When people first came to the United States, it was a nation of beautiful trees and forests. As people settled the land, the trees were cut down to build homes and cities. The number of forests kept getting smaller. Arbor Day reminds us to take care of the earth God has given us. That way there will always be trees for people to enjoy.

We've bought a young tree to be planted today. As we plant, we will pray God's blessing on our work. First, let's pray to God for our tree. *(Have a child pray a prayer of thanks for trees. Then put the tree into the earth.)*

In order for trees to grow, however, we have to plant them in good earth. Then someone has to take care of them. God wants that for all of his creatures, including you and me.

God gives us homes and parents so that we will grow safe and strong. Let's thank God for such care. *(Have a child thank God for all the good things he gives us. Then have children add soil, fertilizer, and water.)*

Now that our tree is planted, we remember that trees are put on this earth for a purpose. They provide shade and homes for animals and birds. They nourish the earth and give beauty to our world. Listen to what the Bible says. *(Read the Bible text.)* Let's pray that God would help us always rejoice in his goodness. *(Have a child pray to close.)*

38. What's in Mom's Briefcase? (Mother's Day)

Note: *Mother's Day is the second Sunday in May.*

Theme: Mothers

Bible Text:

I remember your true faith. That faith first lived in your grandmother Lois and in your mother Eunice, and I know you now have that same faith (2 Timothy 1:5).

Preparation: Put the following items in a briefcase with the word "Mom" taped to the outside: baby toys, diapers, a baby bottle, food cans and boxes, older children's toys, file folders with papers, a duster, kitchen utensils, school books, car keys, an alarm clock, and a Bible.

The Message:

Mother's Day is coming, a very important holiday! Can anyone tell me why? *(Let children respond.)* It's a time to honor and remember our moms. I'm going to ask for a volunteer mom to come forward and help us remember why moms are so important. *(Invite a mom from the congregation to join you.)*

(Form pairs.) Now, we all know that mothers work very hard, so we're loaning our mother a briefcase for her to take to work as mother. Mom, can you take the items out of your briefcase and give one item to each pair. *(After pairs have an item, have them discuss how that item is part of a mother's work.)*

When I mention the item that you've been given, bring it up and put in mom's briefcase. When you were just born, the items that went into mother's briefcase were things like diapers and baby bottles. Why did you need them? *(Let children respond.)* Then you got a little older and mom got you toys. Why are toys important? *(Let children respond.)* Next, you grew a little older and mom could make you grown-up food. Why was that important? *(Let children respond.)* Some moms go to work as well as care for their kids, so some file folders will have to be put into the briefcase. And, of course, there's the house to clean and more meals to cook. Who has some cleaning and cooking supplies?

Then you grow older, and there's school for you. She'll help you with your books, get you up for school (is there an alarm clock out there?), and maybe even teach you to drive. Whew! Look at this briefcase. It's really full! How do you feel about that, Mom? *(Have mother respond.)*

There's just one more thing that we didn't put into the briefcase, though. And it's the most important thing. Let me read from the Bible. *(Read the Bible text.)* Let's put a Bible right on top because God uses mothers to teach us about him. Mothers help keep us strong in the faith. Mothers are one of God's ways of passing on the faith and for that we thank God!

39. A People Church (Pentecost)

Note: *Pentecost falls on the date 50 days after Easter.*

Theme: The church

Bible Text:

When the day of Pentecost came, they were all together in one place. Suddenly a noise like a strong, blowing wind came from heaven and filled the whole house where they were sitting. They saw something like flames of fire that were separated and stood over each person there. They were all filled with the Holy Spirit, and they began to speak different languages by the power the Holy Spirit was giving them (Acts 2:1-4).

Preparation: You'll need a cake for a Pentecost birthday party following the children's message. If possible, bring pictures of church buildings.

The Message:

This is the Day of Pentecost—the day when God sent his Holy Spirit upon his disciples. It's the day the church was born. It's the birthday of the church! Usually when people think of the church, they think of buildings like the one we're in now. Or like this. *(Show pictures of church buildings.)*

But the Holy Spirit came to build another kind of church—a "people church." Let's try to build a people church. I need six volunteers. *(Choose six children—three older, bigger children and three smaller children.)* I want the three biggest kids to get on their hands and knees on the floor. Get very close to one another, shoulder to shoulder, forming a tight line. *(Help the children line up, facing the congregation.)*

Now we need two of the smaller children to get on the backs of these children. *(Have two of the smaller children kneel on the backs of the three bigger children, pyramid style. Invite a few adults to act as spotters who'll help prevent the pyramid from falling in case any children lose their balance.)*

Now we need a steeple for our people church. *(Lift the smallest child onto the backs of the two second level kids. With your assistance, the child should stand, raising hands over his or her head, touching the fingertips to form a steeple.)*

Isn't that a great looking people church? Let's give them a hand! *(Help the children climb down from the pyramid.)* Of course, being a people church doesn't mean making pyramids like this. It means letting God's Spirit live in you and letting others know of God's love for them. Being a people church means living like Jesus lived, helping others in need.

Pentecost is the birthday of the church—the people church. After the service, would you like to have some birthday cake together to celebrate? We can sing a birthday song like this:

Happy birthday to us! Happy birthday to us!

Happy birthday, dear people church!

Happy birthday to us!

We are the people church! Let's sing it together again and thank God for making us his church. *(Sing the birthday song together with the children and congregation.)*

Part Four:
Messages for Summer and All Seasons

40. Summer

Note: *The first day of summer is usually June 21.*

Theme: God's renewal

Bible Text:

The One who was sitting on the throne said, "Look! I am making everything new!" (Revelation 21:5).

Preparation: You'll need a large sign that says "RE-CREATE."

The Message:

It's summertime. Let's have a baseball game. We'll need a pitcher, a catcher, our three basemen, a batter, and some outfielders. I'll be the umpire. *(Set up an imaginary baseball diamond and have kids take their places around it. If there aren't enough children, invite a few adults to join in the game.)*

Play ball! *(Kids will notice there is no ball.)* That's right. You have to play ball with an imaginary ball. OK, pitcher, let's go. *(Lead kids in playing baseball with an invisible ball. Let the first batter get to first base. Then have the second batter strike out.)*

Let's sit down and talk about our game. How did you feel playing this game of invisible baseball? *(Let children respond.)* How do you feel when you play sports in the summer? *(Let children respond.)* What kind of sports do you like to play in the summer? *(Let children respond.)*

There's so much to do in the summer. So much recreation to do.

Recreation really means re-creation. *(Hold up "RE-CREATE" sign.)* Summer is a time when we can be re-created.

God did a fine job creating us the first time, but things like school, homework, jobs, and worry can wear us down and "wreck" us if we're not careful. We need to take time away from our work to play and laugh, to rest and pray. Listen to what the Bible says about God's re-creation. *(Read the Bible text.)*

We need to take the time to rest and turn to God in these summer months so God's Spirit can renew and re-create us. Whatever you plan to do this summer, let God re-create you!

41. Graduation

Note: *Check your local school's calendar to find out when graduation occurs in your community.*

Theme: Lifelong learning

Bible Text:

Wise people can also listen and learn; even smart people can find good advice in these words...knowledge begins with respect for the Lord (Proverbs 1:5, 7a).

Preparation: You'll need gift Bibles or gift books that include Proverbs. Check with your local bookstore.

The Message:

(Have children escort graduates to the front of your church and sit with them. Ask the graduates to each tell what they'll do now that they've graduated.)

Graduation means that you've completed all the requirements to get out of school. But graduation doesn't mean you stop learning.

The book of Proverbs in the Bible was written by wise people. Listen to what Proverbs says about learning. *(Read the Bible text.)*

Wise people will always keep on learning. And they'll begin their learning by knowing how great God is. God's world is so great that we could spend forever learning just a little bit about it. We're proud of you, and we want you to graduate into God's wisdom.

(Have each child take a gift book from you, hand it to a graduate, and shake his or her hand. Then have children and graduates hold hands.)

Let's pray. God, thank you for our graduates. Help them to continue growing in your wisdom. Amen.

42. To Pack or Unpack? (Vacation)

Theme: Rest

Bible Text:
After sending them away, Jesus went into the hills to pray (Mark 6:46).

Preparation: You'll need two suitcases; three signs that read "Work," "Rush-Rush-Rush," and "Worries"; a box of clothes, toiletries, sunscreen, and sunglasses; books (including a Bible), toys, snack food, pen, stamps, and maps. Put the signs in one suitcase, and scatter the clothes and other items around up front. Make sure you have enough items in the box to fill the other suitcase.

The Message:

This is the time of year when many people get ready to go on vacation. It's great to go on vacation, but it's hard to pack for vacation. Let's pretend we're packing for vacation right now. *(Take out the empty suitcase.)*

We've got to pack clothes and sunglasses and sunscreen. Let's find those things and pack them in this suitcase. *(Have children help you collect clothes, sunglasses, and sunscreen. Toss them in the suitcase. Don't be neat about it!)*

We want to have something to do while we're riding in the car or on the airplane, so we better pack some books and toys. *(Have children help you collect books and toys, then toss them in the suitcase.)*

We might get hungry between meals, so of course we'll need to bring some snacks along. *(Have children help you collect snacks and put them in the suitcase.)*

After we get there, we'll want to tell all our friends back home how great it is, so we'll need to take a pen and stamps so we can send them postcards. *(Toss the pen and stamps into the suitcase.)*

Don't forget the maps to take in the car. We might get lost without them! And of course we'll need to take a Bible. *(Toss the maps into the suitcase, then set the Bible on top of the pile.)*

There! I hope we haven't forgotten anything. Now we just have to close our suitcase. *(Try to close suitcase.)* Wow, we sure have a lot of stuff in this suitcase. (Name of child near you), would you mind sitting on this suitcase to help me close it? *(Have a child sit on the suitcase as you close it.)*

We take a lot of stuff with us when we go on vacation. But when Jesus went on vacation, he didn't pack so much. Listen to this Bible verse that tells about Jesus' vacation. *(Read the Bible text.)*

Jesus knew that a vacation was meant to be a time to get close to God and to get away from all the busyness of life. So he just got away—all by himself.

When we go on vacations it's important to pack the things we need. But it's just as important to unpack the things we don't need. *(Hold up the second suitcase.)*

First, we need to unpack our work. *(Take out the "Work" sign, hold it up, then throw it behind you.)*

On vacations we relax and rest. So *(hold up "Worries" sign)* we'll have to unpack our worries. *(Throw the "Worries" sign behind you.)* We worry so much every day. Vacation is a good time to put our worries aside.

Let's also unpack being in a hurry and rushing around. *(Take out the "Rush-Rush-Rush" sign, hold it up, then throw it behind you.)*

On vacation, we'll spend time being quiet. We can pray and read the Bible and watch the hands of the clock go 'round. We can spend time with our families and enjoy each other.

The word "vacation" contains the word "vacate," which means to empty out or to unpack. Jesus didn't take a lot with him when he went on vacation. I hope you can unpack for vacation this year. And when you go on your unpacked vacation, remember to take time to be close to God and one another.

43. How God Made Fathers (Father's Day)

Note: *Father's Day is the third Sunday in June.*

Theme: Fathers

Bible Text:
Since you are God's children, God sent the Spirit of his Son into your hearts, and the Spirit cries out, "Father" (Galatians 4:6).

Preparation: You'll need a cooperative father to demonstrate the fatherly qualities described in this message.

The Message:

Today is Father's Day and I have invited Mr. (father's last name) to help show us what makes a good father. Mr. (father's last name) is (name of child)'s father. (Name of child), thanks for sharing your father with us.

First, a good father must be strong *(father flexes his arms)* so that he can bend down and pick children up, particularly when they're in trouble. *(Have the father pick up his child, then pick up several other children, one at a time.)*

Then, a good father must be smart *(father points to his head)* to teach his children how to stay out of trouble. Next, it's important for a father to have a good strong back so he can give his children piggyback rides. *(Have the father put a child on his back and carry him or her a few steps, then set the child down.)*

Fathers have to know how to smile. *(Father smiles.)* A father's smile says that everything's all right, and children don't need to worry.

Good fathers have big ears, too. *(Father points to his ears.)* That means they can listen to their children. Listening is a very important part of being a father.

But finally, and maybe most important, a good father has a lap. A lap is made when a father sits down *(father sits down)* and makes a seat on his legs for his children. *(Have the father's child sit on his lap.)* Laps are warm and safe places for children to sit, especially when they're tired or sad.

In the Bible, God is often called Father. Listen to what St. Paul says about God being like a father. *(Read the Bible text.)*

That doesn't mean that God is a man. God is God. But we like to think of God as the best kind of father we can imagine. God is strong, God listens to us, God cheers us up when we're sad, and God invites us to come to him when we're tired or discouraged. God gave us fathers to care for us and remind us how much God loves us. That's a very good reason to thank God for fathers today.

Mr. (father's last name), thank you for helping us see how God made fathers. Let's give Mr. (father's last name) and all the fathers in our church a round of applause!

44. Firecrackers (Independence Day)

Note: *Independence Day is July 4.*

Theme: Freedom

Bible Text:
So if the Son makes you free, you will be truly free (John 8:36).

Preparation: You'll need several sheets of bubble wrap. Bubble wrap is used to pack fragile items for moving or shipping. It can be found in many grocery stores or drugstores, as well as in stores that specialize in moving or packaging supplies. Cut the sheets into squares of 12 to 20 bubbles and distribute the squares to the children after they gather. If possible, place a microphone in the midst of the children.

The Message:

The Fourth of July is coming! Independence Day is coming! That means picnics and swimming and singing patriotic songs like "God Bless America." What else do we think of when we think of July 4? *(Let children respond.)*

That's right—fireworks! Lots of places sell fireworks for July 4. Fireworks can be fun if we're safe and careful. But a lot of kids get hurt with fireworks, too. I have some **safe** "fireworks" for us to set off today. They don't require any fire, but they sure make great noises. *(Distribute squares of bubble wrap to the children. Tell them not to pop the bubbles yet.)*

Now, I'd like us to fire off these bubble-wrap "firecrackers," but to do it all together. As I tell you what I know about the Fourth of July, each time I say the word "free" or "freedom," press one of your bubbles and make it pop. Let's practice that. Free. *(Lead children in popping their bubbles. If you have a microphone, encourage kids to gather around it as they pop the bubbles.)*

In the year 1776, a group of people got together to talk about FREEDOM. Our country was ruled by Great Britain in those days, and we weren't really FREE. The people who got together believed that God wanted everyone to be FREE, so they declared their independence. A terrible war was fought so we could have FREEDOM, and now our country is FREE.

As God's people we want to work for the FREEDOM of all people. When people are hungry or homeless, they aren't FREE. We pray for people around the world who aren't FREE. And as Christians, we remember that Jesus came to set all people FREE from sin by his death on the cross. Listen to what Jesus said about FREEDOM. *(Read the Bible text.)*

Let's never forget our FREEDOM—either as citizens of the United States or as Christians. The Fourth of July is a great time to celebrate FREEDOM. We are FREE indeed!

45. Freedom Sharing (Independence Day)

Note: *Independence Day is July 4.*

Theme: Freedom

Bible Text:
We have freedom now, because Christ made us free (Galatians 5:1a).

Preparation: None necessary.

The Message:

July 4 is coming. What's so special about July 4? *(Let children respond.)* July 4 is Independence Day! On that day we remember that in 1776 our country declared its independence from Great Britain, and we became a free nation.

Let's play a game to see what we can do with our freedom. I'd like our big kids to form a circle and hold hands. Next I'd like two smaller kids to get inside the circle. *(Pause to allow the circles to form.)*

Smaller kids, your job will be to get out of the circle. Big kids, you'll try to keep them in the circle. Let's see how you do. Go! *(Let the smaller kids try to get out. Applaud kids' efforts no matter what the results.)*

Now, what if we asked three of our big kids to get inside the circle with the smaller kids? Let's see what happens! *(Have three big kids join the smaller kids in the circle, then have all the kids inside the circle try to get out. Keep adding big kids to the inside until kids are able to break through the circle. When the circle has been broken, applaud kids' participation, then have them return to their places.)*

Freedom is a great gift of God. As a free nation we want others to be free, too. Just as those big kids helped their smaller friends break free from the circle, our nation looks for ways to help others in the world to be free.

As God's Christian people we've been set free by our Lord Jesus. Listen to what the Bible says. *(Read the Bible text.)* We want others to know about Jesus' love so that they can be free from sin and know the freedom that Jesus brings.

When you're free, you want to share your freedom with others. Let's remember that on this Independence Day!

46. Happy Day! (Birthdays)

Theme: You're special

Bible Text:

I always thank my God for you because of the grace God has given you in Christ Jesus (1 Corinthians 1:4).

Preparation: You'll need a ribbon, a birthday cake, forks, a knife, napkins, and paper plates. You can use this message to celebrate one child's birthday or several children's birthdays.

The Message:

It's (name of child)'s birthday on (date) and that is a special day, indeed. How many of you here will have a birthday this year? *(Show of hands.)*

Of course, you all will! That was a silly question because everyone who is born has a birthday. Birthdays are a time to remember the special day you were born and the difference you make in this world. So, let's take a few moments to think of (name) and give thanks to God for (name).

There are over 5 1/2 BILLION people in the world! That's a lot of people. But (name), you're special—there is only one of you! And there is no one quite like (name). Nobody looks, talks, thinks, or loves exactly the way (name) does. Out of all the 5 1/2 billion people of this world, there is only one (name).

Listen to the way St. Paul thanked God for some special people that were part of his life. *(Read the Bible text.)*

We give thanks to God for you, (name), for all you do and for all you are, and for all the ways God's love comes through in you. You're a special gift to us. As a matter of fact, I think we should gift-wrap you just to remind you that you're God's gift to us. *(Have kids help you put a ribbon around the birthday child's chest.)*

I also brought a cake to help us celebrate later. But for now, let's sing "Happy Birthday" to (name). On the second verse we'll sing:

You're God's gift to us.
You're God's gift to us.
Thank God for you, (name),
You're God's gift to us.

(Lead the congregation in singing "Happy Birthday," using the second verse printed above. After the service, serve birthday cake.)

47. Souvenirs (Weddings)

Theme: Love

Bible Text:
I will tell about the Lord's kindness and praise him for everything he has done (Isaiah 63:7a).

Preparation: Do this children's message with the permission of the bride and groom. Have the guest book as part of the message with a ballpoint pen for the children to use in signing their names. Wrap a simple gift cross for the wedding couple in a box. Make sure the children can unwrap it quickly.

The Message:

Isn't this a beautiful time? Look at all the people here for this wedding service. Some of them have traveled a long way because they love (bride and groom) and want to be part of this special day.

What do you notice about weddings that is different from our regular church services? *(Let children respond.)* All of those things say that this is a very special service, and one that (bride and groom) and all of us will remember for years.

It's important to remember days like this, and sometimes we have souvenirs to help us. A souvenir is a reminder that an event happened. When you look at the souvenir, it brings back good memories. These wedding rings *(show rings)* are the most important souvenirs of today for (bride and groom). Every time they look at their hands, they'll remember this day.

I'm going to ask you to give (bride and groom) a souvenir—a reminder—that you were here. Sign your name on this special children's page of the wedding book as we talk now. *(Pass the guest book and pen around.)*

I have another souvenir for (bride and groom.) Could someone help me open this box? *(Have a child open the box.)* This cross will be a souvenir for them, too. A cross reminds us that Jesus loves us and died for us so that our sins can be forgiven. A cross reminds us that we can forgive one another and try to love one another just as Jesus loves us. A cross reminds us that we need Jesus to help us have happy homes.

(Retrieve the guest book after all children have signed it.) Thank you for your souvenir signatures. One last thing we'd like to do is pray for our bride and groom. *(Pray for God's blessings on the marriage.)*

48. Hugs and Hallelujahs (Funerals)

Note: *Funerals can be confusing, even frightening events for children. You can give this message before a funeral or memorial service to prepare children for the occasion, or adapt it slightly, and give it during a funeral or memorial service.*

Theme: Death

Bible Text:

The angel said to the women, "Don't be afraid. I know that you are looking for Jesus, who has been crucified. He is not here. He has risen from the dead as he said he would. Come and see the place where his body was" (Matthew 28:5-6).

Preparation: None necessary.

The Message:

On (date of funeral or memorial service) many of us will attend a funeral for (name of deceased). How many of you have ever been to a funeral before? What was it like? *(Let children respond.)*

Funerals can be very sad occasions, because we're sad that (deceased) has died. So if you come to the funeral, you might notice that many people are crying. You might feel like crying, too, and that's OK. Crying is one way people can express their sadness at a funeral.

We have funerals for two reasons: for hugs and hallelujahs. You'll see a lot of hugs at a funeral because people need to help each other when a loved one dies. Sometimes hugs are the best way to help one another. Hugs say, "I care about you and want you to feel better."

At the funeral, we'll talk about how good (deceased) was and how much we'll miss (deceased). But sometimes we won't know what to say, so we'll hug each other. *(Hug a child sitting near you.)* So if you're going to the funeral on (date of funeral), be sure to bring your hugs.

The other reason we go to funerals is for hallelujahs. Hallelujah is an old word that means "praise the Lord." Sometimes we say hallelujah at Easter time to praise God for Jesus' resurrection. Let's say it together now. *(Lead kids and congregation in saying "hallelujah!")*

89

Jesus' followers were sad when they went to his tomb on Easter morning. It was like going to a funeral. But listen to what happened when they got there. *(Read the Bible text.)*

When we go to a funeral we praise God for Jesus. Because Jesus rose from the dead, (deceased) and all of us can be with Jesus forever in heaven. Knowing that (deceased) is with Jesus makes us very happy. That makes us want to say "hallelujah!"

So when you go to the funeral on (date of funeral), you'll see some people who are very sad. You might feel very sad yourself. You might want to get or give some hugs.

But then we'll all remember that Jesus rose from the dead on Easter and we'll say "hallelujah." Remember to bring your hugs and hallelujahs with you to the funeral!

49. Thank a Teacher (Teacher Appreciation Days)

Theme: Teachers

Bible Text:
Choose my teachings instead of silver, and knowledge rather than the finest gold. Wisdom is more precious than rubies. Nothing you could want is equal to it (Proverbs 8:10-11).

Preparation: You'll need a bushel of apples.

The Message:

(Have teachers come forward with the children.)

Let's form a long chain. *(Have everyone hold hands and form a long line.)* Be careful because there are lots of things that can break the chain. If the chain is broken, your grandchildren may not have teachers to teach them about God's Word.

(Walk down the line and say the following phrases. As you do, pretend to try to break the chain.)

I'm too tired to go to church.

I don't have time to teach.

I don't believe in God anymore.

I'd rather watch TV.

Let somebody else do it.

Wow! Your chain is so strong. Turn to a teacher and thank him or her for being faithful to teach you what he or she has learned about God. If they had used any of these excuses, you may not have learned all the things you have about God and his Word. *(Pause while children thank their teachers.)*

When we say thank you to someone, we're saying that what they do is important to us. And teachers are very important. Listen to what the Bible says about teaching. *(Read the Bible text.)*

We have a big bushel of apples for our teachers, and I'd like each child to grab an apple and find his or her teacher. Give your teacher a hug and an apple as a way of showing that you appreciate him or her. *(Allow time for kids to give hugs and apples.)*

Thank you, teachers!

50. "Get Your Bible" Days

Note: *Many churches give Bibles to children when children reach a certain age. If your church gives out Bibles, use this message on that occasion.*

Theme: The Bible

Bible Text:

All Scripture is given by God and is useful for teaching, for showing people what is wrong in their lives, for correcting faults, and for teaching how to live right (2 Timothy 3:16).

Preparation: You'll need Bibles to give to the children. You'll also need a hammer, a nail, and a piece of wood.

The Message:

I've got to hammer this nail into this wood before we can have our children's message. *(Hammer the nail using the wrong end of the hammer. Keep hammering and hamming it up until kids correct you.)*

What? What was I doing wrong? *(Let children respond.)* I guess I wasn't using the hammer the way it was designed to be used, was I? Tools need to be used appropriately to get the best use out of them.

Today is a very important day for you. It's the day that our church gives you a very important tool for your faith—the Bible. We believe God speaks to us in the Bible, so we want everyone in our church to have a Bible, especially our children. Listen to what the Bible says about itself. *(Read the Bible text.)* God uses the Bible like a tool to build us up, to fix us up, and to keep us living the way he wants us to. The Bible also tells us how much Jesus loves us, how God forgives us, and how we have a home with God in heaven forever. I can't think of anything more important. If you have a valuable tool, you've got to use it!

So when we give you this Bible today, we'd like you to use it.

Let's pray that God will bless you as you read and follow his Word. *(Close with a prayer similar to this one.)* Thank you, God, that you speak to us through the pages of this wonderful book. Help us always to turn to its message for our daily living and help us remember what a great gift it is to us. May we use these Bibles well, so we can be the kind of people you want us to be. We ask your blessing on them. In Jesus' name, amen. *(Distribute the Bibles.)*

51. We're All Adopted!

Theme: Adoption

Bible Text:
Because of his love, God had already decided to make us his own children through Jesus Christ (Ephesians 1:5).

Preparation: You'll need a cross and party treats. This message is designed to celebrate an adoption. Before the message, talk with the adopting family about showing the legal adoption documents to the children and talking about the adoption.

The Message:

Today we're very happy because the (name of family) have just completed the adoption of (name of child). Who knows what adoption means? *(Let children respond.)*

Sometimes when children are born, their birth parents decide that they must let their children be raised by other parents. That happens for a lot of reasons. But God provides lots of wonderful adopting parents to raise these children. The adopting parents promise to love and care for their adopted child just as though that child were born to them.

(Have the adoptive parents tell why they adopted their child. Then have them show the official adoption papers.)

If anyone wonders whether (name of child) is the child of (name of parents), they can check these papers to prove it. But the papers aren't really what's important to either the parents or the child; it's the love and care that lets them know they're a family.

We don't know what the future will bring in this family any more than we know what the future will bring for any of our families. But we do know that their love will always be there.

When the Bible tells us how much God wants to love us, it says that God wants to adopt us! All of us! Listen. *(Read the Bible text.)* How many of you want to be adopted by God? *(Let children respond.)*

God doesn't give us papers to let us know that we're adopted. God gives us a cross! *(Hold up the cross.)* God let his Son die for us on the cross! The cross of Jesus is our adoption certificate. Place your hand on this cross or on someone who is touching the cross. *(Pause for children to respond to your instruction.)* At the count of three, let's all say, "I'm adopted!" OK? One, two, three. *(Lead children in saying "I'm adopted!")*

Whenever we look at the cross of Jesus and know how much he loves us—so much that he died for us—we can say "I'm adopted!" Just like (name of child).

Today as we celebrate (name of child)'s adoption, we remember that we are all adopted by God! And that's something to celebrate. *(Pass out treats to celebrate the child's adoption.)*

52. Saying Goodbye

Theme: Moving away

Bible Text:
Let the Lord watch over us while we are separated from each other (Genesis 31:49b).

Preparation: You'll need large self-stick note pads or adhesive-backed name tags and markers.

The Message:

Today is a sad day for us and for our friend (name of child). (Name)'s family has been with us for a while, and this week they're moving to another city. That means we won't have them with us in Sunday school or church, and we're going to miss them. How does it feel when you miss being with somebody? *(Let children respond.)*

But today is also a happy day, because we know God will be with them in their new home. They'll be meeting new friends and having lots more good times.

Let's think of what we can give (name) as a going-away present. I've given you each a piece of paper. It's one of those sticky-back papers. I'd like you to write your name on the side that's not sticky. *(Hand out markers.)* I'll give you a moment to do that while I read you a verse from the book of Genesis. *(Read the Bible text.)*

This is a good "goodbye" verse for us when friends leave us. Even though (name) will be far away, God will still be watching (name), and he'll still be watching all of us, too.

(Name), we want you to remember the friends you have here. *(Have the child who's moving stand in the middle of the group. Have the rest of the children number off from one to four.)* Let's have these kids put their names on your shirt. *(Have the ones stick names on the front of the child's shirt or dress.)* Keep these friends always in your heart.

Now, we'll ask these kids to put their names on your back and shoulders. *(Have the twos stick their names on the child's back and shoulders.)* Remember that these friends will always be patting you on the back and cheering for you even if they're miles away.

How about if these kids put their names on your legs? *(Have the threes stick their names on the child's legs and feet.)* We'll be standing with you wherever you go.

And finally, hold out your arms and let your friends put their names on your arms and hands. *(Have the fours stick their names on the child's arms and hands.)* We hope the friendship and love we've shared with you in Jesus' name has made you strong for the years ahead.

Well, (name) looks a little strange wearing all our names. I'll bet (name) will want to take them off pretty soon. But (name), the love and prayers we have for you will stick to you forever. No matter how old you get or how far you go, we'll always be a part of your life. "Let the Lord watch over us while we are separated from one another."

(If you'd like, close this message by praying for the child and family who'll be moving.)